8.95

# KIDDING ™
## *Around*

## CLEVEL

A FU

TI

Santa Fe, New Mexico

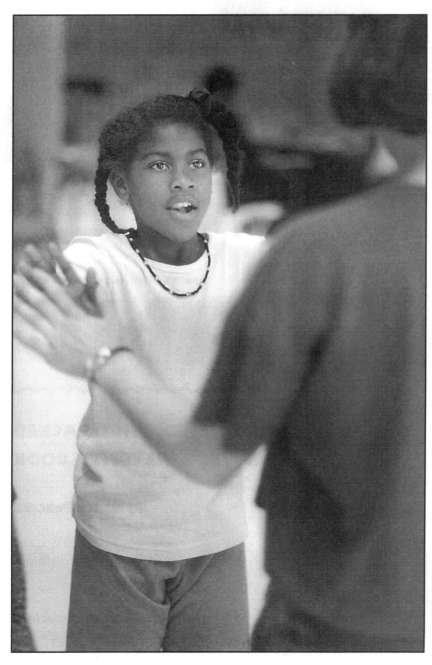

John Muir Publications
P.O. Box 613, Santa Fe, NM 87504

Printed in the United States of America
First edition. First printing February 1997

Library of Congress Cataloging-in-Publication Data
Peacock, Nancy.
    Kidding Around Cleveland: a fun-filled, fact-
packed travel & activity book/by Nancy Peacock.—
1st ed.
        p.        cm.
    Includes index.
    Summary: Provides information on landmarks,
museums, parks, sports activities, entertainment,
restaurants, and more things to see and do in the
Cleveland area.
    ISBN 1-56261-335-9 (pbk.)
    1. Cleveland (Ohio)—Guidebooks—Juvenile
literature.  2. Family recreation—Ohio—
Cleveland—Guidebooks—Juvenile literature.
[1. Cleveland (Ohio)—Guides.] I. Title.
F499.C63P43  1997                    96-47353
917.71'320443—dc21                    CIP
                                      AC

**Editors** Dianna Delling, Lizann Flatt
**Production** Nikki Rooker
**Graphics** Tom Gaukel
**Typesetting** Marcie Pottern
**Cover Design** Caroline Van Remortel
**Cover Photo** © Andre Jenny/Unicorn Stock Photo
**Back Cover Photo** Jim Baron/The Image Finders
**Illustrations** Stacy Venturi-Pickett
**Maps** Susan Harrison
**Printer** Burton and Mayer

For photo credits, see page 139.

Distributed to the book trade by
Publishers Group West
Emeryville, California

*Although the author and publisher have made every
effort to provide accurate, up-to-date information, they
accept no responsibility for loss, injury, or inconvenience
to any person using this book.*

# C O N T E N T S

# COLOR THE ROUTE
# FROM YOUR HOMETOWN
# TO CLEVELAND

If you're flying, color the states you'll fly over. If you're driving, color the states you'll drive through. If you live in Ohio, color the states you have visited.

# 1  WELCOME TO CLEVELAND!

YOU'RE STANDING ON PUBLIC SQUARE. LOOK UP! All around you, rising up into the clouds, you see the giant skyscrapers of downtown Cleveland. Now look down. In 1800, this sidewalk was a green pasture where cows and horses grazed. Finally, look around you. You see statues, pigeons, city buses, taxicabs, and cars, but mostly you see people—hundreds of people! People crossing the streets, relaxing on park benches, and hurrying to or from somewhere or other. Cleveland is one busy city.

↑ **The Terminal Tower and Society Center buildings**

The city was built where the Cuyahoga River meets Lake Erie, one of the five Great Lakes. This region is called the North Coast of the United States because four of the five Great Lakes form the border between the U.S. and Canada.

## HOW TO USE THIS BOOK

If you are planning a trip to the Cleveland area, this book can be very helpful. Each chapter is filled with kid-friendly, interesting things to see and do. This book describes greater Cleveland's parks, animals, landmarks, sports teams, recreation areas, museums, entertainment, shopping, food, and festivals.

Read each chapter before you visit Cleveland. Make a list of the places you would most like to visit. Share this list with other people in your family. Remember to include places that all of you can enjoy. Then use the addresses and phone numbers in the Resource Guide. Many of the sites listed will send free maps and brochures ahead of time.

Using the journal pages found at the end of each chapter, write down where you went and what you did. This is a great way to remember your trip.

⬆ **The Cuyahoga River runs west of downtown Cleveland.**

## THAT'S CLEAVELAND WITH AN "A"

Moses Cleaveland was a Revolutionary War captain from Connecticut. After the war, he joined the Connecticut Land Company in buying the land south of Lake Erie. In those days, that area of land was called the Western Reserve. It was the westernmost part of the United States.

In 1796, Cleaveland and about 40 others journeyed through the wilderness of New York and Pennsylvania. They reached the mouth of the Cuyahoga River on July 22. Immediately, they began to lay out a city that would be the capital of the Western Reserve. In October, Cleaveland and most of his group went back to Connecticut, never to return.

Although he never wanted to live here, Cleaveland was proud of the new town. He even bragged that someday Cleveland would be as big as Old Windham. At the time, Old Windham had a population of 2,700. Today, greater Cleveland's population is 1.5 million.

⬆ **Moses Cleaveland founded Cleveland in 1796.**

## PUBLIC SQUARE

When Moses Cleaveland and his surveyors created the city, they marked off a 10-acre public square at the center. This grassy field was used to graze farm animals. Today, the only animals on Public Square are the many pigeons that stroll the sidewalks and a few horses that pull open-air carriages.

One thing hasn't changed, though. Public Square is still the heart of Cleveland. The tallest buildings in the city ring the square, and it is still a center for outdoor concerts, parades, and special ceremonies.

⬆ **Public Square sits at the center of the city.**

# DRAW YOUR OWN BUILDING

What would you build if you could build anything you wanted?
In the space between the buildings, draw your ideal house, skyscraper,
or office building. When you're done, color in the page.

## CARTER'S CABIN

At first, no one wanted to live in Cleveland because the land near the mouth of the Cuyahoga River flooded easily. Settlers complained of getting sick from the swamp. What they didn't know was that the bites from swamp mosquitoes were giving them a disease called malaria.

Finally, a Vermont settler named Lorenzo Carter came to Cleveland and stayed. His cabin was used for a trading post, a post office, a school, and a church. Today, you can see a replica of that cabin. It is now surrounded by warehouses and bridges, on the banks of the Cuyahoga River.

↑ A replica of Carter's Cabin sits on the banks of the Cuyahoga.

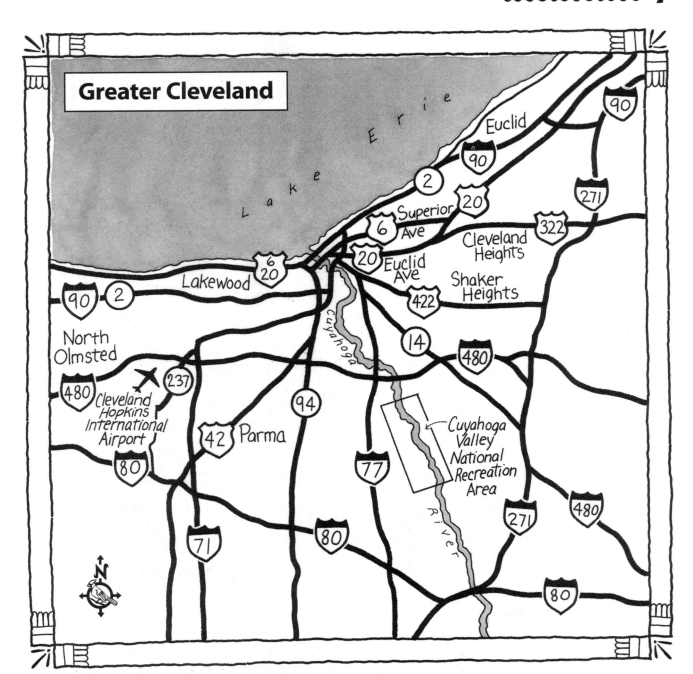

## CLEVELAND'S ETHNIC PRIDE

When Cleveland became a center for trade in the mid-1800s, Irish, German, and Scottish people came to fill the new jobs. A second wave of immigrants (people from other countries) in the late 1800s brought people from Italy, Poland, Yugoslavia, Hungary, and Slovenia. Then during the two World Wars, African Americans came north from the southern states to take war-time jobs. After Europe was torn apart by World War II, many homeless Europeans came to Cleveland. The most recent wave of immigrants was from India, Africa, and Southeast Asia.

⬆ **Irish residents love the annual St. Patrick's Day Parade.**

**According to local lore, at one time Cleveland had more Hungarians than any other city outside of Hungary.**

What does all this ethnic diversity mean for Cleveland? There are festivals every month of the year celebrating different ethnic or religious heritages. People share their food, art, dancing, and other traditions. So check the Calendar of Events at the back of this book and take part in the color and excitement of Cleveland's many cultures.

# ON THE ROAD TO CLEVELAND

**People from many countries have
moved to Cleveland in the past 100 years.
Can you unscramble the names of the countries below?**

NFARCE    _____

EANYMRG    _____

AINDI    _____

INAHC    _____

DOLNPA    _____

TAYIL    _____

NARHUGY    _____

## FAMOUS CLEVELANDERS

Jesse Owens was a senior at East Tech High School in Cleveland when he ran the 100-yard dash in world-record time, 9.4 seconds. "He didn't run, he floated," wrote *New York Times* sportswriter Arthur Daley. "He was the prettiest runner I ever saw."

While writer Jerry Siegel and artist Joe Schuster were still students at Glenville High School in 1933, they created Superman, the comic book hero. Superman went on to star in a 1950s TV series and several theater movies. He's still popular today.

Margaret Hamilton, who played the Wicked Witch of the West in *The Wizard of Oz* movie, was from Cleveland. Her sister Dorothy was married to the son of Cleveland inventor Charles Brush, who created the electric street light.

## WEATHER

Cleveland has four distinct seasons. The summers are mild with plenty of sunny days

⇑ **Jesse Owens claimed the world long-jump record for 25 years.**

for swimming and boating. Out-of-towners come to Cleveland in the fall just to see the spectacular red, orange, and gold leaves on the trees. Winters are cloudy but fun, with enough snow for sledding and skiing. Spring officially arrives when the buzzards return to Cleveland, their northern roosting spot.

**Other famous Clevelanders:**
- **Actress Halle Berry**
- **Entertainer Arsenio Hall**
- **Actress Debra Winger**
- **TV comedian Drew Carey**
- **Astronaut James Lovell**

# JESSE OWENS BREAKS THE TAPE

**Jesse Owens won four gold medals at the 1936 Olympics in Berlin, Germany. He was also a native of Cleveland. Color in this scene, which shows young Jesse winning a race.**

## THE COMEBACK CITY

At the end of World War II, Clevelanders began to move out of the city to the suburbs. Stores, restaurants, movie theaters, and even factories moved to the suburbs, too. By the late 1960s, downtown Cleveland was full of old, empty buildings. No one wanted to go downtown anymore. Pollution in the Cuyahoga River was so bad that the chemicals in the river actually caught fire! Some people called Cleveland "The Mistake on the Lake."

But then things started to change for the better. In the 1980s, new skyscrapers were built on Public Square. More jobs were available downtown. Old buildings were turned into new restaurants. The Cuyahoga River was cleaned up and the riverfront area was turned into the Flats, a fun place where people could sail boats and dine on the patios of outdoor restaurants.

Today Cleveland is called "The Comeback City" because of all the new activities happening around town. The Rock and Roll Hall of Fame and Museum and the Great Lakes Science Center are two of the newest attractions that bring visitors to Cleveland's North Coast Harbor. The Gateway Sports Complex is the new home of Cleveland's professional baseball, basketball, and hockey teams. There has never been a better time to visit Cleveland. Enjoy your visit to the Comeback City!

**The Flats remains an important industrial area in Cleveland.** ⇨

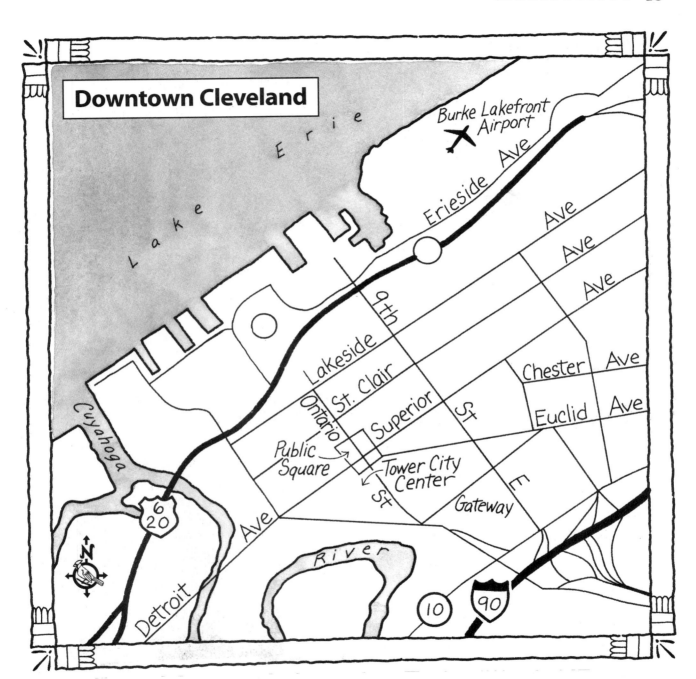

# 2 PARKS AND THE GREAT OUTDOORS

GETTING OUT OF DOORS IS important and lots of fun. You know how great it feels to race through fields, splash in a fountain or lake or stream, or relax in the shade of an oak tree. You can do all of those things in Cleveland.

The Cleveland Metroparks, the Cuyahoga Valley National Recreation Area, and all the state parks along the shores of Lake Erie provide plenty of activities for burning off extra energy. Rockefeller Park Greenhouse and the Cleveland Botanical Gardens have outdoor gardens for warm weather, and indoor displays for wintry days.

**Relaxing on the beautiful grounds of the Holden Arboretum**

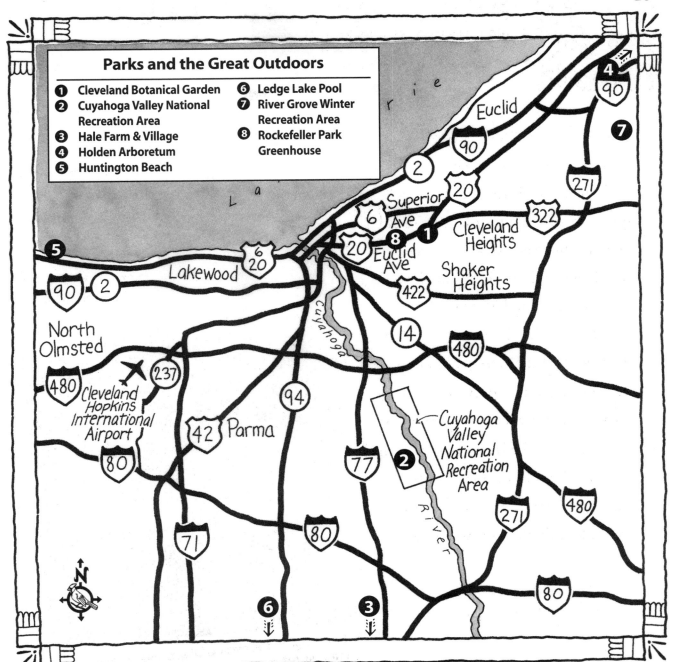

## Parks and the Great Outdoors

1. Cleveland Botanical Garden
2. Cuyahoga Valley National Recreation Area
3. Hale Farm & Village
4. Holden Arboretum
5. Huntington Beach
6. Ledge Lake Pool
7. River Grove Winter Recreation Area
8. Rockefeller Park Greenhouse

# CLEVELAND METROPARKS

The Cleveland Metroparks form an "emerald necklace," surrounding greater Cleveland with 19,000 acres of valleys, gorges, and rivers. You can bike, walk, run, and in-line skate on the 60 miles of paved all-purpose trails. Exercise on any of the eight physical fitness trails, fish or boat in one of six lakes, or swim at **Huntington Beach** or in **Ledge Lake Pool**.

When snow begins to fall, go skiing at the Cross-country Ski Center in the **River Grove Winter Recreation Area** of the North Chagrin Reservation. Skiers can also use the unpaved hiking trails and the paved all-purpose trails of all Cleveland Metroparks.

**Toboggan fun at Mill Stream Run** ⇧

**From November through February, you can ride a toboggan down a 1,000-foot refrigerated chute at Mill Stream Run.**

# TOBOGGAN TRIP

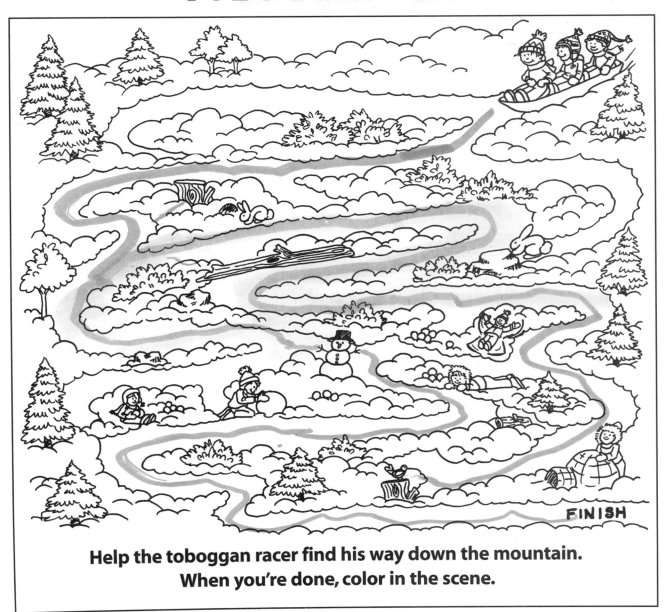

**Help the toboggan racer find his way down the mountain.
When you're done, color in the scene.**

FINISH

# CUYAHOGA VALLEY NATIONAL RECREATION AREA

This park stretches 22 miles between Cleveland and Akron, along the path of the old **Ohio & Erie Canal**. You can still see parts of the canal when you visit. The **Tow Path Trail** is a 20-mile walking or biking trail that takes you past an old stone lock. The trail signs explain how the lock worked like an elevator to raise and lower the boats. The **Canal Visitors Center** is a historic building where boat passengers passing through Lock 38 bought food and supplies.

You can rent a bike in the town of **Peninsula** or hike part of the **Buckeye Trail**, a 1,200-mile trail that passes through the park. You can see turtles basking on rocks and great blue herons catching fish in the marshes. White-tailed deer, Canada geese, and beavers live here, too.

⇧ Biking along the canal

The 312-mile Ohio & Erie Canal was finished in 1832. Horses walked along a tow path, pulling boats in the canal behind them.

# MIXED-UP PICTURE STORY

This picture story should show a boat going through the old Ohio & Erie Canal. Unfortunately, the pictures are out of order. Put the scene in the correct order by filling in the number box in the bottom left-hand corner of each picture.

# HOLDEN ARBORETUM

An arboretum is a place where trees, shrubs, and plants are grown and studied. To find your way through this 3,100-acre outdoor museum, start at the **Visitors Center**. Borrow a backpack with an audio tape for a self-guided tour of the **Blueberry Pond Trail** and **Sensory Trail**, or take a tour with a guide. Outdoor grills and picnic tables make it fun to bring a lunch or snack. Spend time in the **Butterfly Garden** or the **Wildflower Garden**. From mid-September to mid-October, the 20 miles of trails become a fairyland of color with red, orange, and gold leaves.

In winter, follow animal tracks in the snow. During the month of March, watch as buckets of sap from maple trees are turned into maple syrup at the **Sugarbush & Museum**.

🌲 Guides are happy to teach visitors about nature at the Holden Arboretum.

**Take a look at the red oak tree in Holden's Rhododendron Garden. The tree is more than 275 years old.**

# HIDE AND SEEK!

Draw a circle around each hidden object in this garden. When you're done, color the scene. Look for: bunny face, bone, drum, bird, bell, bear, clock, hot dog, apple, pencil, heart, pie slice, bread, spoon, baseball, airplane, face.

# HALE FARM AND VILLAGE

Hale Farm was started by Jonathan Hale in 1827. In the 1950s, the Western Reserve Historical Society used some of the farm pastures to create a village. Historic buildings from all over northeast Ohio were taken apart, shipped to Hale Farm, and put back together.

Now the village has several historic houses, a church, a law office, a log schoolhouse, a sawmill, glassworks, and a smokehouse. Gardens and farm buildings are laid out just as they would have been in the mid-1800s.

Skilled craftspeople in costumes show how to shoe horses, spin wool, dip candles, and blow glass. The park is open from June through October, but you can see a special Winter Holiday Festival in December, and Maple Sugaring Days in February and March.

⇧
**This old-fashioned churn turns cream into butter.**

**Kids wear clothes from the ⇒
1800s at Hale Farm.**

# AN 1800S VILLAGE WORD SEARCH

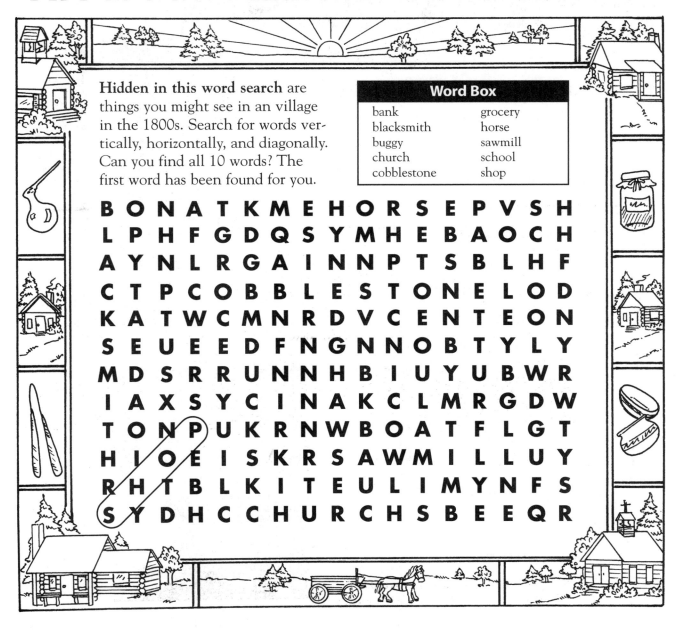

**Hidden in this word search** are things you might see in an village in the 1800s. Search for words vertically, horizontally, and diagonally. Can you find all 10 words? The first word has been found for you.

### Word Box

| | |
|---|---|
| bank | grocery |
| blacksmith | horse |
| buggy | sawmill |
| church | school |
| cobblestone | shop |

```
B O N A T K M E H O R S E P V S H
L P H F G D Q S Y M H E B A O C H
A Y N L R G A I N N P T S B L H F
C T P C O B B L E S T O N E L O D
K A T W C M N R D V C E N T E O N
S E U E E D F N G N N O B T Y L Y
M D S R R U N N H B I U Y U B W R
I A X S Y C I N A K C L M R G D W
T O N P U K R N W B O A T F L G T
H I O E I S K R S A W M I L L U Y
R H T B L K I T E U L I M Y N F S
S Y D H C C H U R C H S B E E Q R
```

**⇧ A peaceful garden spot**

**⇧ Greenhouses allow tropical plants to grow in Cleveland.**

# ROCKEFELLER PARK GREENHOUSE

Have you ever seen or heard a talking garden? Rockefeller Park Greenhouse has one. It's called the **Talking Garden for the Blind.** When you walk close to the garden plants, herbs, and displays, tape-recorded messages describe them. Betty Ott, one of the first American women to become a radio talk-show star, lived in Cleveland in the 1950s. She was the driving force in getting the garden built.

The outdoor **Japanese Garden** has a path with a little wooden bridge. There are several wishing ponds, so be sure to bring enough pennies for all your wishes.

The greenhouse has an acre of tropical plants, ferns, cacti, and orchids. On a rainy afternoon or a cold winter day, this colorful and steamy plant habitat is a great place to stop and smell the orchids.

# COLOR TO FIND THE ANSWER

You can see one of these in the Japanese Garden at Rockefeller Park Greenhouse. Color the shapes with numbers in them brown. Color the shapes with letters in them blue. Color the other shapes any colors you want.

# CLEVELAND BOTANICAL GARDEN

Take time from your busy schedule to enjoy the Cleveland Botanical Garden. You can walk through a fancy **English Garden** of herbs and plants used for spices or medicines. The **Japanese Rock Stream Garden** was planted on a hillside so it looks like the flowers, grasses, and rocks are rushing down the hill like water. The library has a reading garden with benches and a gazebo for outdoor relaxing. Discover the secret life of plants with special interactive exhibits. The indoor **winter holiday displays** are a Cleveland tradition.

**Year-round children's programs at the Cleveland Botanical Garden include making Japanese screens, Easter eggs, Passover plants, and a worm bin.**

⇑ **The Japanese Rock Stream Garden**

⇐ **Summer flowers in bloom**

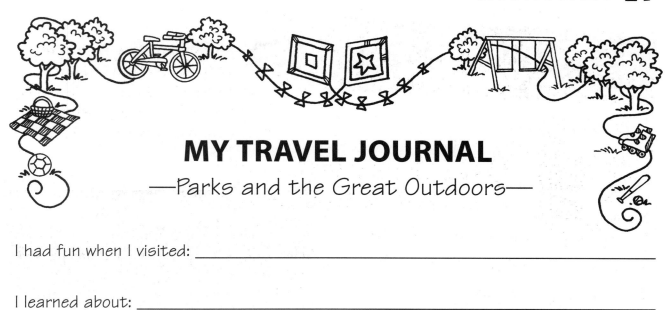

# MY TRAVEL JOURNAL
## —Parks and the Great Outdoors—

I had fun when I visited: _____

I learned about: _____

My favorite park was: _____


This is a picture of what I saw at a park in Cleveland

# 3 ANIMALS, ANIMALS

NO MATTER WHERE YOU ARE IN Cleveland, animals are not far away. The Cleveland Metroparks Zoo and Rain Forest is home to more than 3,300 animals. You can visit educational farms or a marine life park with enough animals to fill an ocean.

If you're visiting in mid-March, don't miss Buzzard Sunday in Cleveland Metroparks Hinckley Reservation. Every year, flocks of buzzards return from their winter homes in the south to the cliffs, caverns, and open fields of Whipp's Ledges here. Bring your binoculars.

Any time of year, you can hear the song of cardinals, goldfinches, and many other birds. Deer, raccoons, opossums, skunks, groundhogs, rabbits, ducks, and geese can be found throughout the Cleveland Metroparks.

⬆ **Watch the whales swim at Sea World of Ohio.**

**Animals Around Cleveland**

1. Burnette's Farm and Educational Center
2. Cleveland Metroparks Zoo & Rainforest
3. Lake Erie Nature and Science Center
4. Lake Farmpark
5. Ralph Perkins Wildlife Memorial Woods Garden
6. Sea World of Ohio

# LAKE ERIE NATURE AND SCIENCE CENTER

On the west side of Cleveland, the Lake Erie Nature and Science Center in Bay Village has a wonderful collection of white-tailed deer, foxes, water and land turtles, opossums, red-tailed hawks, groundhogs, owls, turkey vultures (known locally as buzzards), and wild turkeys. The collection also includes a saltwater tank of sea life and a freshwater tank of Lake Erie fish. The center has pets like guinea pigs, ferrets, rabbits, and chinchillas, and exotic animals including iguanas, boa constrictors, and pythons. Call ahead for the schedule of live animal programs. You may get the chance to pet a skunk, hold a turtle, or stroke a 20-foot python.

↟ **Open-roofed pens allow close-up viewing.**

↟ **Welcome to the Nature and Science Center!**

# HOW TO FIND ANIMALS

If you want to see animals in the wild, Ken Gober, Senior Naturalist at the Rocky River Nature Center, has these suggestions:

- Choose the right time of day. Mornings and evenings are the most active time for animals because they are looking for breakfast or they are looking for that last bite of food before going to sleep.

- Choose the right location. Try to find a place where two habitats come together—where the edge of a forest meets a meadow or where a swamp or pond meets a field, for example.

- Be quiet, move slowly, and be patient. Try not to point or shout when you see an animal.

# RALPH PERKINS WILDLIFE MEMORIAL WOODS GARDEN

On the east side of Cleveland, a good place to see wild animals is the Ralph Perkins Wildlife Memorial Woods Garden at the Museum of Natural History. Bald eagles, hawks, owls, foxes, raccoons, and deer live here because they were injured and cannot survive in the wild.

This woodsy setting looks just like the animals' original forest home. They are fed and protected here. The garden also protects plants, including 100 wildflower specimens, shrubs, and trees.

Every weekend afternoon, museum staff and volunteers present live animal programs that educate and delight visitors. Visitors can handle one of the animals at the end of the program.

Unlike most birds, buzzards (turkey vultures) don't have a voice box. Their calls are mostly hisses and grunts.

⇡ **Bald eagles live peacefully in this woodsy setting.**

# WHERE DO THEY LIVE?

**By tracing the tracks of each animal, can you discover who each den belongs to?**

# CLEVELAND METROPARKS ZOO

A visit to the zoo is like a whirlwind tour of the world. The **African Plains** area has the largest herd of Masai giraffes in the country, as well as antelopes, zebras, and lions. **Monkey Island** is home to graceful Colobus monkeys, with their flowing manes of black and white hair.

Cold weather animals live in the **Northern Trek** area. You can see polar bears, brown bears, sea lions, and camels. The newest exhibit in this area is **Wolf Wilderness**. The wolf pack shares this forest habitat with bald eagles, beavers, and fish.

Spend some time with the gorillas in the **Primates, Cats, & Aquatics** building. Watch the two toddlers, Little Joe and Okpara, and the four adults: Brooks, Bebac, Mokolo, and Joe.

⬆ **Zebras are native to Africa.**

**Free trams at the zoo carry you from one area to another.**

⬅ **Tigers can weigh more than 600 pounds!**

# CROSSWORD FUN

You can see and do a lot at the Cleveland Metroparks Zoo.
Solve this crossword by figuring out the clues or completing
the sentences. If you need some help, use the clue box.

## Across

2. This animal can balance a ball on her nose.
4. Furry, white polar _____s come from the arctic regions.
6. The animal with the longest neck in the zoo.
7. A ferocious animal may be kept in a _____.
8. This "king of the beasts" roars loudly.

### Clue Box

| | |
|---|---|
| lion | snake |
| cage | gorilla |
| feed | giraffe |
| seal | bear |
| elephant | |

## Down

1. The _____ can swing his long trunk.
2. Scales cover the body of this slithering reptile.
3. This large, hairy animal is a type of ape.
5. Zoo employees _____ the animals.

# THE RAIN FOREST

The **Rain Forest** exhibit at the **Cleveland Metroparks Zoo** is designed to look like rain forests in Africa, Asia, and South America. This steamy, tropical indoor jungle is home to 600 animals and 10,000 plants. Your tour begins at a 25-foot waterfall and continues through dense foliage, past a scientist's hut, and into a walk-through aviary that is home to sloths, capybaras, and giant anteaters. Further down the path are natural displays that feature ocelots and clouded leopards.

You can see thousands of rain forest insects, including leaf-cutting ants, hissing cockroaches, and walking sticks. You can even look into the eyes of a 12-foot crocodile. The scariest exhibits of all are the ones that explain how quickly the rain forests are being destroyed.

⇡ The Jungle Cascade at the Rain Forest Exhibit

Every 12 minutes, a tropical rainstorm—complete with thunder and lightning—blows through the zoo's Rain Forest exhibit.

# CONNECT THE DOTS

**Connect the dots to find a rain forest creature. Then color the scene.**

# BURNETTE'S FARM & EDUCATIONAL CENTER

For the past 50 years, Dr. Jim Burnette has taken in orphaned or injured animals from Cuyahoga County. He also raises exotic animals from around the world. You'll see lots of animals on a tour of his farm, from lambs, goats, and bunnies to deer and ducklings. See aracuna chickens that lay colored eggs and silky chickens with fur-like feathers. The farm also has Barbary apes, tree raccoons, miniature horses, pot-bellied pigs, and peacocks.

Most of Dr. Burnette's animals are bottle-fed and hand-raised. Bring fruits, vegetables, or bread to feed the animals. You can stand in the gazebo or on a small bridge and feed the koi (a type of fish originally from Japan).

The farm also has flower gardens and a pavilion picnic area. Pony rides cap off the hour-long tour.

These animals have found a home at Burnette's Farm. ⇒

# FUNNY STUFF AT THE FARM

**Without telling anyone what you're doing, ask for a word to fill in each blank. For example, "Give me an action word." When all the blanks have been filled in, read the story out loud. One blank has been filled in for you.**

Farmer _____ was tired of growing corn and _____s.
        boy's name                                vegatable

He decided to plant mystery seeds on his farm instead. One

spring morning he put on his _____ socks _____ and scattered the
                              article of clothing

_____ seeds in his field. Each day he watered the seeds
describing word

with _____ and waited to see if they would grow. At
     liquid or beverage

first he saw only _____ plants poking out of the ground.
                  describing word

But soon his plants were big and _____. The farmer
                                 describing word

harvested his plants in the fall and sold them at _____
                                                   name of store

for _____ dollars per pound. He was the only farmer in
    number

_____ who had grown his own _____!
name of town                       food

## LAKE FARMPARK

Do you know what the main ingredient of white bread is? If your answer is wheat, you're right. If you didn't know, don't feel bad. Nearly half of all Americans don't know, either.

Almost everything we eat still comes from a farm. In 1800, about 90 out of every 100 people lived on farms. Today, only three out of every 100 people live on them.

From husking corn to milking a cow, you can try your farming skills on the 235 acres of Lake Farmpark. You can visit with dozens of types of lambs, pigs, chickens, ostriches, horses, mules, and goats. Help plant potatoes in the spring and taste vegetables and fruits in the summer. In the fall, help make apple cider and take a horse-drawn wagon ride.

⇑ **This farmer is using a horse-drawn plow.**

**At a Lake Farmpark exhibit called the Great Tomato Works, you can see a model of a tomato vine with 6-foot tomatoes and 12-foot leaves.**

# WHAT'S WRONG HERE?

**This might look like Sea World of Ohio, but it's not.**
**Circle 14 things that you think are wrong with this picture.**
**When you're done, color the scene.**

# SEA WORLD OF OHIO

How would you like to have a close encounter with a killer whale or a dozen Atlantic sharks? You can do both at Sea World, which is home to animals from oceans around the world.

**Patagonia Passage** is an outdoor pool with banks that look like the rocky coastline of South America. This habitat is home to penguins and dolphins.

**Dolphin Cove** is a 375,000-gallon tank where you may have the chance to touch and feed bottlenose dolphins.

At **Shamu Stadium**, killer whales Shamu and Namu leap and splash through the water with their trainers.

At **Shark Encounter**, you can ride a moving walkway offering exciting views of sand-tiger, brown, nurse, and lemon sharks.

⇑ **A killer whale and its trainer at play**

⇑ **Penguins frolic in Patagonia Passage.**

# MY TRAVEL JOURNAL
## —Animals Around Cleveland—

I had fun when I visited: _____

I learned about: _____

_____

My favorite animal was: _____

This is a picture of an animal I saw

# 4 LANDMARKS, SKYSCRAPERS, AND THE ARTS

IF YOU GO SIGHTSEEING IN CLEVELAND, you will have some curious sights on your list. For example, there is an enormous red sculpture in Willard Park next to City Hall. Famous sculptor Claes Oldenburg created this piece of art to look just like a huge hand stamp that prints the word "FREE."

A sculpture at the corner of East Ninth Street and Euclid Avenue is called *Triple L Eccentric Gyratory III*. It is a large, moving, metal mobile that turns with the wind so it always looks slightly different each time you see it. Many murals are painted throughout the city on the sides of buildings.

To get an unusal view of the city, take a ride up the Terminal Tower skyscraper to the observation deck. The city looks very different from 600 feet in the air!

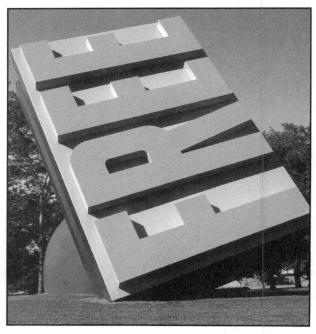

⇑ **This Willard Park sculpture is hard to miss!**

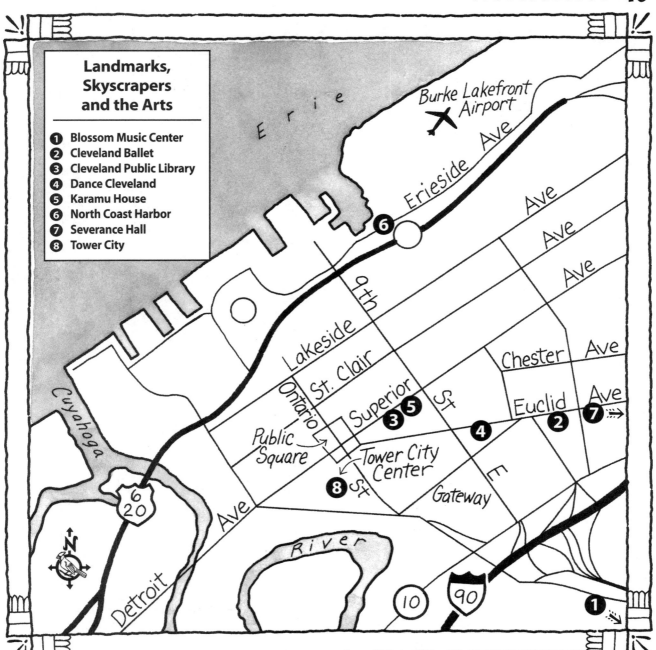

**Landmarks,
Skyscrapers
and the Arts**

1. Blossom Music Center
2. Cleveland Ballet
3. Cleveland Public Library
4. Dance Cleveland
5. Karamu House
6. North Coast Harbor
7. Severance Hall
8. Tower City

# LOLLY THE TROLLEY

One of the easiest, fun-filled ways to see Cleveland is on Lolly the Trolley. Lolly is a bright red trolley on wheels who takes her passengers on tours of the city's most interesting sights.

On the one-hour tour, Lolly takes you to **North Coast Harbor**, home of the Rock and Roll Hall of Fame and Museum, the Great Lakes Science Center, the USS *Cod* submarine, the *William Mather* ore freighter, and Burke Lakefront Airport. Visit downtown sights like riverfront restaurants at the Flats, the Warehouse District, and Ohio City.

On the two-hour tour, you'll see all those sights, plus you ride along Lake Erie's coastline and you'll see Playhouse Square and University Circle. A few well-behaved kids get to ring Lolly's clang-clang-clang bell at the end of the tour.

↑ **Lolly drives past the Garfield Memorial.**

**Lolly the Trolley has driven nearly 3 million miles taking passengers around the city.**

# CONNECT THE DOTS

**Using one of these vehicles, you can see the sights of Cleveland.
Connect the dots to catch one, then color in the scene.**

# TOWER CITY

**Tower City comes alive during the holidays.**

Tower City is a collection of hotels, stores, restaurants, movie theaters, and a train station. It's like one big city under a huge roof. On the bottom level of this mammoth building is **Tower City Station**, an RTA terminal on the Greater Cleveland Regional Transit Authority's public transit system.

Rapid transit trains go west to Cleveland Hopkins International Airport and east to University Circle, Shaker Square, Green Road, Van Aken Boulevard, and East Cleveland. The newest rapid train line is the Waterfront Line, which takes passengers to Settler's Landing in the Flats and North Coast Harbor on Lake Erie.

One level above the RTA train station is the **Avenue at Tower City**, a shopping mall of unusual stores, restaurants, and movie theaters.

Above that, take a ride up to the observation deck of the Terminal Tower to see what Cleveland looks like from 57 stories in the air.

**The Terminal Tower, seen through a Tower City skylight**

# HIDE AND SEEK!

**Draw a circle around each hidden object in the train station. When you're done, color the scene. Look for: hourglass, cup, beehive, paintbrush, baseball, lizard, toothbrush, piece of candy, snail, teddy bear, heart, face, water pitcher, baseball bat, birthday cake**

# CLEVELAND PUBLIC LIBRARY

You might not think that a library would be part of a sightseeing trip. But wait until you see the Cleveland Library. The main building, which opened in 1930, has white marble staircases that are so pretty you won't want to ride the elevator. The chandeliers, painted murals, and decorated ceilings will make you think you are in a millionaire's mansion.

Take time to browse through the children's room. Two fully furnished antique dollhouses are on display. Or look at the dozens of chess sets from the **John White Collection**. It's the largest collection of chess sets and books in the world.

The new $90-million Louis Stokes Wing is an ultra-modern, rounded building with lots of windows. It will be completed in 1998.

In 1890, Cleveland was the first large city library to let people take books off the shelves themselves. Before that, librarians brought books to the library vistors.

**← The Cleveland Library's Louis Stokes Wing**

# LOOKING AROUND THE LIBRARY

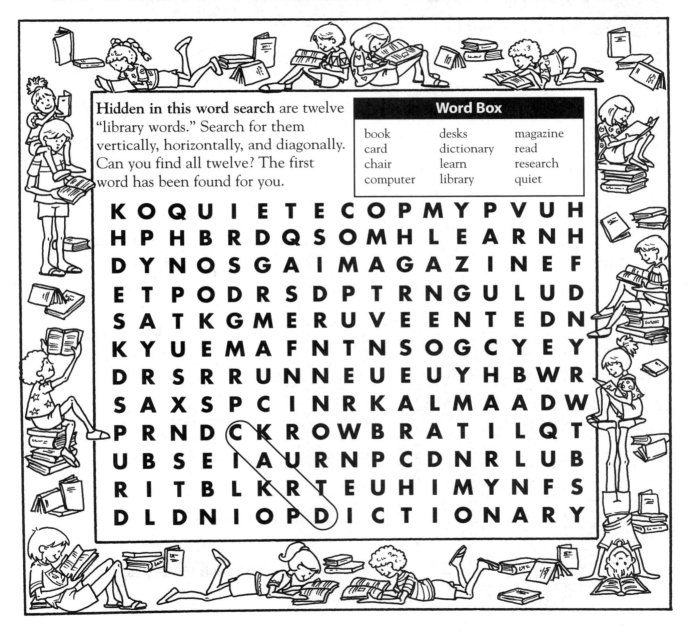

Hidden **in this word search** are twelve "library words." Search for them vertically, horizontally, and diagonally. Can you find all twelve? The first word has been found for you.

**Word Box**

| | | |
|---|---|---|
| book | desks | magazine |
| card | dictionary | read |
| chair | learn | research |
| computer | library | quiet |

K O Q U I E T E C O P M Y P V U H
H P H B R D Q S O M H L E A R N H
D Y N O S G A I M A G A Z I N E F
E T P O D R S D P T R N G U L U D
S A T K G M E R U V E E N T E D N
K Y U E M A F N T N S O G C Y E Y
D R S R R U N N E U E U Y H B W R
S A X S P C I N R K A L M A A D W
P R N D C K R O W B R A T I L Q T
U B S E I A U R N P C D N R L U B
R I T B L K R T E U H I M Y N F S
D L D N I O P D I C T I O N A R Y

# KARAMU HOUSE

*Karamu* is a Swahili word meaning "a place of joyful gathering," and that's exactly what Karamu House is. It's also the oldest American theater producing plays written by African Americans. It was started in 1915 by a young couple who wanted to encourage harmony among the African American, Austrian, Italian, Russian, Jewish, Syrian, Chinese, and other immigrants who lived on Cleveland's east side. Every year, Karamu presents a series of plays. During the Christmas season, Karamu actors perform Langston Hughes' **Black Nativity**, a celebration of gospel, dance, and theater. The Karamu House has more than just two theaters. The complex also houses art galleries, dance studios, classrooms, a day-care center, and a community bank. Children's art classes take place on Saturdays.

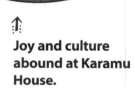

⇧
**Joy and culture abound at Karamu House.**

**In 1918, Karamu House held its first play—*Cinderella*. All parts were played by kids.**

# WHAT'S THE DIFFERENCE?

These two pictures of people at the Karamu House may look the same, but they're not. Can you find at least 15 differences between the two scenes?

# CLEVELAND DANCE

Dance in Cleveland can be many things. If you enjoy classical ballet with dazzling costumes and majestic sets, the **Cleveland Ballet** can supply all three. Each Christmas the company performs *The Nutcracker* with all the trimmings.

The Cleveland Ballet also presents such classics as *Romeo and Juliet*, *Swan Lake*, and *Coppelia*. The company performs in **Playhouse Square Center** in Cleveland and in its sister city of San Jose, California.

**DanceCleveland** is a group that brings contemporary dance companies to Cleveland. These companies combine jazz, modern, tap, and ballet movements in new and different ways. DanceCleveland also puts on young people's concerts that are entertaining and educational.

↥ **The Cleveland Ballet's performances are magical.**

# THE DANCE CONTEST

Without telling anyone what you're doing, ask for a word to fill in each blank. For example, "Give me an action word." When all the blanks have been filled in, read the story out loud. One blank has been filled in for you.

_____ was one of _____ girls and boys entering
　　　girl's name 1　　　　　　　　　　　　number

the dance contest. Her partner, _____, was a _____
　　　　　　　　　　　　　　　　boy's name 1　　　　　　describing word

dancer. He had a _____ costume that was _____ with
　　　　　　　describing word　　　　　　　　　　color

_____ polka dots. _____'s favorite dance was to
　color　　　　　　　　boy's name 1

_____ around the room and act like a _____.
　action word　　　　　　　　　　　　　　　　thing

On the day of the contest, the couple danced for _____
　　　　　　　　　　　　　　　　　　　　　　large number

hours straight. Their dance was so _____*crazy*_____ that the audience
　　　　　　　　　　　　　　　　describing word

roared with laughter, but they still won the contest!

# CLEVELAND ORCHESTRA

The Cleveland Orchestra is one of America's finest orchestras. From September through May, conductor Christoph Von Dohnanyi leads the orchestra in concerts at **Severance Hall** on University Circle. Severance Hall looks like a white marble palace.

In the summer, the orchestra heads south to Cuyahoga Falls near Akron. The orchestra's summer home is the **Blossom Music Center**, an open-air concert stage surrounded by 150 acres of rolling woodlands. You can sit either in numbered seats under the enormous shell roof or on a grassy hillside. Families bring picnics, listen to the orchestra play, and watch the stars twinkle overhead.

⬆ **Conductor Christoph Von Dohnanyi**

**Enjoy art and fresh air at the Blossom Music Center.**

**The orchestra plays music for kids of all ages. There are special concerts for students and families throughout the year.**

# MY TRAVEL JOURNAL
## —Landmarks, Skyscrapers, and the Arts—

I had fun when I visited: _____

I learned about: _____

My favorite building was: _____

This is a picture of a building I saw

# GOOD SPORTS

SPORTS ARE A VITAL PART OF CLEVELAND'S CULTURE.
The Indians have been Cleveland's baseball team since
1901. From fall through spring, fans go
indoors to root for the Cavaliers
basketball, Lumberjacks hockey, and
Crunch soccer teams.

If you like to play sports yourself,
there are lots of opportunities. Lake
Erie provides plenty of water and
beaches for swimming, boating,
water-skiing, and sailing.

Cleveland Metroparks have
19,000 acres of parkland for hiking,
horseback riding, cross-country
skiing, tobogganing, jogging, biking,
golfing, fishing, in-line skating,
swimming, and more.

↥ **Jacobs Field, home of the Cleveland Indians**

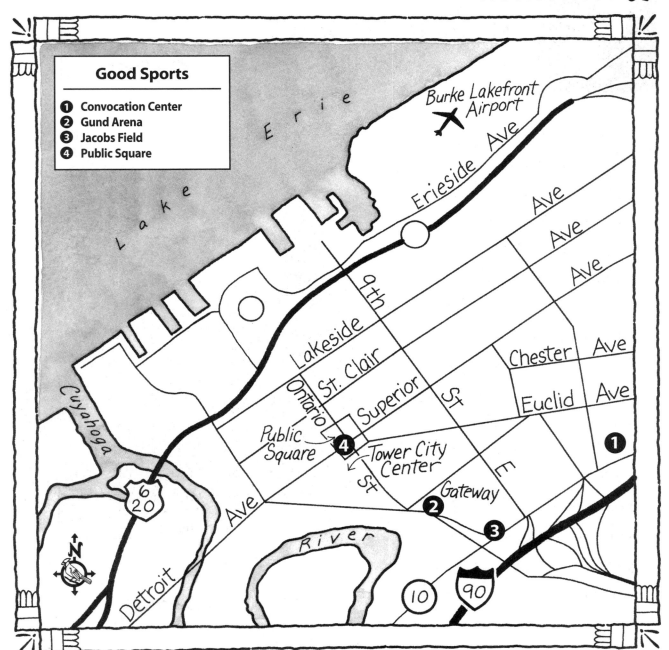

**Good Sports**

❶ Convocation Center
❷ Gund Arena
❸ Jacobs Field
❹ Public Square

# THE CLEVELAND INDIANS

The Cleveland Indians were the 1995 American League Champs. They have so many fans that every ticket for the 1996 and 1997 seasons sold out before the season started. **Jacobs Field** opened in 1994, and it's one of the finest baseball stadiums in the country. Younger kids can play in the **Kid's Land** play area. A special concession stand sells peanut butter and jelly sandwiches and juice boxes. The snow cones and cotton candy are just a dollar each. Nearby, kids have their own gift shop with kid-friendly prices.

The concourse has interactive batting games that put you in the middle of what looks like Jacobs Field. There is a speed-pitch machine and a booth where you can turn your photo into a baseball card.

On your way to Jacobs Field, stop at the Peterson Nut Company for snacks of nuts and candy. The store is located on the corner of Carnegie and E. Ninth Streets.

↑ **Fans love the Indians!**

# WHAT'S IN COMMON?

**Each of these baseball players has something in common with the two others in the same row. For example, the top row of players are all wearing their hats backwards. Draw a line through each row and describe what the players in that row have in common. Don't forget diagonals!**

# THE CLEVELAND LUMBERJACKS

At the start of each game, the Lumberjack's mascot Buzz skates onto the ice or drops from the top of the arena on ropes.

The Lumberjacks ice-hockey team loves kids! So bring your ice skates to a Lumberjacks home game at **Gund Arena**. After an action-packed Friday-night game, fans of all ages are invited to skate on the ice. Several of the players skate with you and sign autographs. It's a fun way to meet the players and Buzz, the Lumberjacks' beaver mascot.

You can even celebrate your birthday with the Lumberjacks. The Lumberjacks will provide a birthday cake, your favorite player will sign a Lumberjacks T-shirt, and Buzz will visit you in your seat before the game.

In August, the Lumberjacks hold a hockey camp and a roller hockey tournament.

Lumberjacks hockey games are always lively events.

# HIDE AND SEEK!

**Draw a circle around each hidden object in this hockey game. When you're done, color in the scene. Look for: watermelon slice, mushroom, cane, water pitcher, boomerang, bucket, television, sailboat, pencil, baseball, typewriter, boot, mouse, ruler, clock**

# CLEVELAND CAVALIERS

From November to April, the Cleveland Cavaliers take on the Bulls, Pistons, Magic, and other NBA teams in Gund Arena.

Whammer, the Cav's bear mascot, loves to shake kids' hands. You can watch instant replays on the four big Arenavision video screens over center court and during time-outs—the FanCam picks out young fans and flashes their pictures up on the video screen. So wear a funny hat, paint your face, or bring a homemade sign to wave in the stands. You might see your face on the big screen!

**It would take more than 53 million basketballs to fill Gund Arena.**

⬆ **The Cavaliers play in Gund Arena.**

# CROSSWORD FUN

**Solve this basketball crossword by figuring out the clues or completing the sentences. If you need some help, use the clue box.**

## Across

2. The playing area in basketball is called a _____.
5. Before the game begins, fans sing the national _____.
6. This hangs from the hoop.
7. Players who are not in the game sit on this wooden plank.

## Down

1. If you make a basket you score these.
3. The Cavaliers are my favorite basketball _____.
4. He's the Cavaliers' mascot.
8. Another name for the game of basketball.

### Clue Box

| | |
|---|---|
| anthem | net |
| bench | points |
| court | team |
| hoops | Whammer |

# CLEVELAND CRUNCH

If you love a great soccer game, go see the Cleveland Crunch. The 1996 Champions of the National Professional Soccer League play in the **Convocation Center** at Cleveland State University. During breaks between quarters, team members throw official Crunch miniature soccer balls to their fans. At home games, the announcers tell you which two players will be signing autographs after the game. Bring your program or something else to get an autograph.

You can also sign up for the Revco Crunch kids program. You get tickets, a T-shirt, and after-game autograph sessions with the whole team at two "Kids Night at the Crunch" home games.

⬆ **The 1996 champions**

⬅ **Crunch fans are a rowdy bunch.**

# MATCH THE MATES

**Find each player's teammate by matching up the uniforms each player is wearing. When you're done, color in the scene.**

# SPORTS FOR YOU

There are more than 15 rinks in Greater Cleveland for indoor ice skating. During the Christmas holidays, the city of Cleveland puts in an outdoor ice rink on **Public Square**. Skate at night with the holiday lights twinkling around you.

For biking, jogging, hiking, and in-line skating, ride the 60 miles of paved trails in the **Cleveland Metroparks**. The city also has a long list of recreation centers that offer tennis and both indoor and outdoor swimming.

From May through September, spend a Sunday afternoon with the **Cleveland Polo Club** in the Cleveland Metroparks South Chagrin Reservation. In between polo matches, you can go onto the field and press the hunks of sod kicked up by the horses back into place.

⇑
**Cyclists in the Cuyahoga Valley National Recreation Area**

**Skaters enjoy the season on Public Square.**
⇛

# MY TRAVEL JOURNAL
—Good Sports—

I had fun when I visited:

_____

I learned about: _____

My favorite sport is: _____

This is a picture of something I saw

# 6 MUSEUMS AND MORE

IN ANY CITY, MUSEUMS TELL A LOT about what is important to the people who live there. In Cleveland, music is important. There is one museum for rock and roll and another for polka. Cleveland has other museums for trolley cars, ore boats, cars, submarines, airplanes, and spacecraft. Whether you like ancient artifacts or cutting-edge art, dinosaur bones or shooting stars, bridges or big teeth, Cleveland is sure to have a museum that will interest you.

At Trolleyville U.S.A., you can ride historic trolleys around a restored railroad track. You'll discover what an old train station looked like. There is also a picnic area, so bring a lunch or snack.

⬆ The USS *Cod* submarine offers public tours.

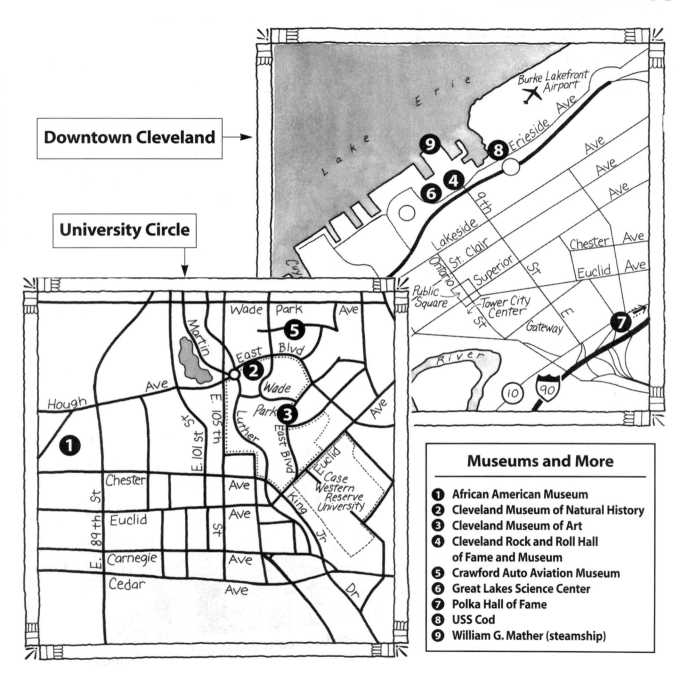

**Downtown Cleveland** →

**University Circle**

**Museums and More**

❶ African American Museum
❷ Cleveland Museum of Natural History
❸ Cleveland Museum of Art
❹ Cleveland Rock and Roll Hall of Fame and Museum
❺ Crawford Auto Aviation Museum
❻ Great Lakes Science Center
❼ Polka Hall of Fame
❽ USS Cod
❾ William G. Mather (steamship)

# GREAT LAKES SCIENCE CENTER

Become a human gyroscope! Analyze your own baseball bat swing, try out virtual reality, or meet Zelda, the zebra mussel. The Great Lakes Science Center has 350 interactive exhibits, allowing visitors to explore physical science, computer technology, the environment, and much more.

The six-story, silver dome of the museum also houses the **Cleveland Clinic OMNIMAX Theater**. Take a hair-raising trip down white-water rapids or blast into outer space. The theater uses the most advanced sound system and film projection system in the world.

**The Great Lakes Science Center, with Lake Erie in the background**

**The Great Lakes Science Center is one of the eight largest hands-on science centers in the United States.**

# HANDS-ON SCIENCE

**Hidden in this word search** are some things you might see or do at a science museum. Search for words vertically, horizontally, and diagonally. Can you find all 8 words? The first word has been found for you.

**Word Box**

| | |
|---|---|
| magnet | Omnimax |
| atoms | science |
| electric | theater |
| experiment | weather |
| fun | Zelda |

```
K O N A T K M E S O P M Y P T U H
H E H F R D Q S Y M H E B A H N H
N L N L S G A I N N P T S B E T F
T E X P E R I M E N T N G U A U D
R C T W G M A R D V C E N T T D M
D T U E M D F N G N N C G T E E A
E R S R L U G N H U I N Y E R W G
S I X E P C F N D K C E M R A D N
P C Z D U K U O O M N I M A X Q E
U I S E I S N R N P Y C N L L U T
R O T B L K I T E U L S M Y N F S
A T O M S O P Y F W E A T H E R R
```

# CLEVELAND MUSEUM OF NATURAL HISTORY

Dinosaurs, insects, people, animals, and precious gems—how did we all end up sharing this planet? The Cleveland Museum of Natural History wants you to feel the rumble of an earthquake and the heat of volcanic lava. Touch rock walls and crystal formations. Meet Happy, the 70-foot *Haplocanthosaurus delfsi* dinosaur skeleton that is 150 million years old. He shares the **Hall of Prehistoric Life** with prehistoric fish and two meat-eaters: a 40-foot *Allosaurus* and a "pygmy tyrant" *Nanotyrannus*.

On a clear evening, get close-up views of the moon, stars, planets, and faraway galaxies through the public observatory's telescope. Or see some shooting stars in the planetarium show.

In 1974, one of the oldest fossil skeletons of a human ancestor was discovered in Africa by a curator of Cleveland's Museum of Natural History.

⇛
**This giant roams the Hall of Prehistoric Life.**

# WHAT'S MISSING HERE?

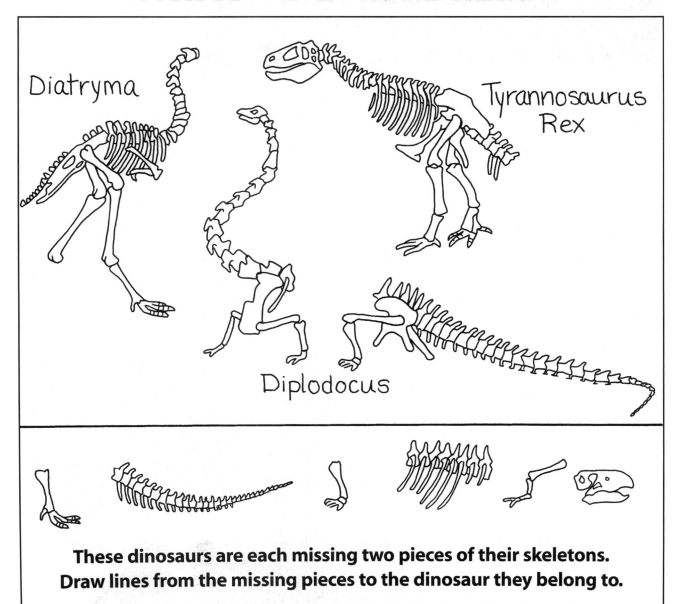

Diatryma

Tyrannosaurus
Rex

Diplodocus

**These dinosaurs are each missing two pieces of their skeletons.
Draw lines from the missing pieces to the dinosaur they belong to.**

# CLEVELAND ROCK AND ROLL HALL OF FAME AND MUSEUM

The Rock and Roll Hall of Fame and Museum looks like an eight-story glass pyramid. It was designed by the famous architect I.M. Pei and cost $92 million to build.

Inside the museum, guests can follow the living history of rock 'n' roll music. The exhibit hall is filled with the colorful costumes of rock's wildest performers. Shop for CDs, tapes, and souvenirs at the museum's **HMV Music Store**. Or take a break from the exhibits and relax in the museum's café. You'll enjoy spectacular views of the surrounding North Coast Harbor.

On a sunny day, take time to hang out on the sprawling plaza in front of the museum. There is a garden filled with plants and outdoor speakers designed to look like rocks that play music. Get it? Rock music!

**This museum is impressive both inside and outside.**

**If you have time, visit the Polka Hall of Fame, located in the Shore Cultural Center in Euclid.**

# HIDDEN MESSAGE

**Cross out the J's, P's, W's, U's, X's, and B's.**
**The letters you have left spell out a secret message.**

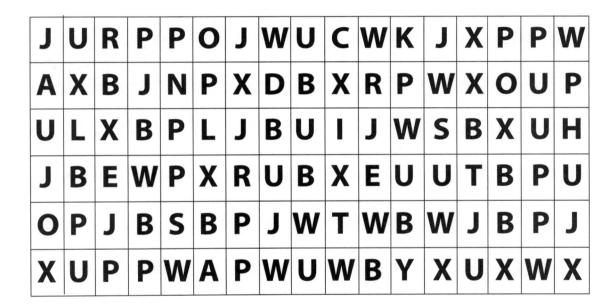

**Write the hidden message here:**

# FLOATING MUSEUMS IN NORTH COAST HARBOR

↥ Visitors tour the steamship *William G. Mather.*

The *William G. Mather* is 618 feet long—5 yards longer than two football fields. The *Mather* is twice the length of the USS *Cod*!

If you like to climb ladders and squeeze through small spaces, you will enjoy a tour of the **USS** *Cod*. The *Cod* was one of 200 submarines in the South Pacific during World War II. Today it is the only sub that is still in its original condition and in the water. The three ship keepers, who will sell you tickets and answer your questions, all served on submarines during World War II. Climb aboard and enter the forward torpedo room. Peer through a periscope and aim a 5-inch gun.

The steamship **William G. Mather** was the flagship of the Cleveland Cliffs Steamship Company's line of ore freighters. The ship was built in 1925 and hauled iron ore, grain, stone, and coal for 55 years. Tours of the *Mather* take you through the huge cargo holds, the crew's quarters, and the engine room. You can also see the fancy dining room and staterooms where wealthy passengers stayed.

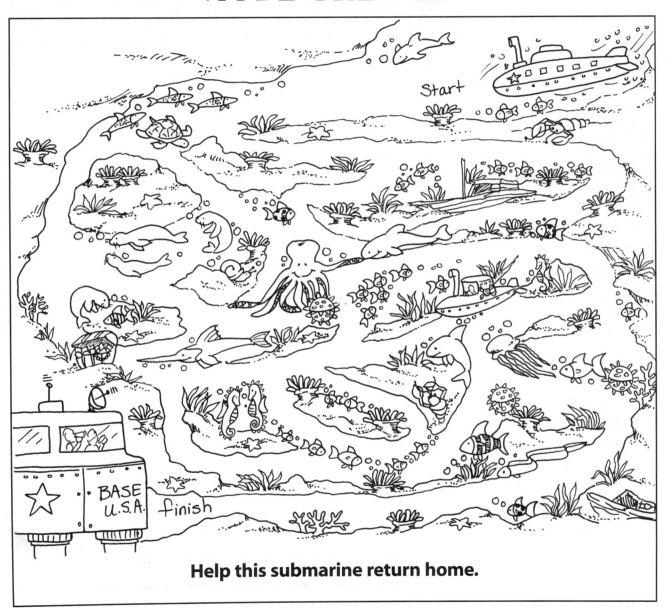

# SAVE THE SUB!

**Help this submarine return home.**

# CRAWFORD AUTO-AVIATION MUSEUM

Cleveland, not Detroit, was the "motor city" when cars were first manufactured. From 1896 to 1932, 80 different kinds of cars were made in Cleveland. Many of those cars are in the Crawford Auto-Aviation Museum in University Circle.

The museum displays more than 150 automobiles, bikes, and aircraft. The oldest car in the museum is a French-made 1897 *Panhard et Lavassor*, which has candles for headlights. You can see steam-powered and electric cars. The museum also has the limousine used by Presidents Johnson, Nixon, Ford, and Carter. Check out the bulletproof glass windows that are half an inch thick.

⇑ **See turn-of-the-century cars at the Crawford Auto-Aviation Museum.**

**A reporter for the *Cleveland Plain Dealer* newspaper was the first American to call a "horseless carriage" an automobile.**

# WHAT DOESN'T BELONG?

**You'll see cars like these at the Crawford Auto-Aviation Museum.
Use crayons to color and decorate them.**

# CLEVELAND MUSEUM OF ART

↑ Monet's *Water Lilies* is one of the museum's most famous paintings.

One of the world's great art museums sits on a 15-acre park called the **Fine Arts Garden** in University Circle. The white marble building opened in 1916 and now houses 30,000 works of art in 70 galleries.

Explore the **Armor Court**, a gallery devoted to suits of armor, swords, daggers, and other interesting medieval weapons. Browse through the museum's enormous collections of Asian, Mayan, African, European, and American weapons.

When you get tired of art appreciation, get a snack or meal from the museum's restaurant. In good weather, you can enjoy your food at a table in the **Outdoor Sculpture Courtyard**.

← The museums offers special art classes for kids.

Remember not to touch any of the artwork at the museum. Over time, touching the art will damage the surface of a painting or the smoothness of a sculpture.

# APPRECIATE ART!

**Hidden in this word search** are some things you might see or learn about at an art museum. Search for words vertically, horizontally, and diagonally. Can you find all 12 words? The first word has been found for you.

| Word Box | | |
|---|---|---|
| art | drawing | painting |
| bench | frame | sculpture |
| bronze | gift shop | sketch |
| cafe | marble | vase |

```
S K E T C H T E F R A M E P V U S
H P H K T D Q S O M H L E A R N C
D Y V R S G A I M A G A Z I N E U
P T A O D R S D R A W I N G L U L
A A S B G M E R U V E E N P E D P
I Y E E M A F N T N S O O C Y E T
N R S B R B N N E U E H Y H B M U
T A X R P E I N R K S L M A A A R
I R N O C N R O W T R A T I L R E
N B S N I C U R F P C D N R L B B
G I T Z L H R I E U H I M Y N L S
D L D E I O G D I C T I C A F E Y
```

# AFRICAN AMERICAN MUSEUM

To find out the history of African Americans in Cleveland and throughout the United States, visit the African American Museum. You'll see the original stoplight invented by Cleveland's genius inventor Garrett Morgan. Morgan also invented the gas mask. He saved many lives when he wore it to rescue injured miners trapped in an explosion. The **Science Corner** has hands-on exhibits on famous black scientists from George Washington Carver to astronaut Guyenne Blueford.

The **African Room** highlights different regions of the continent, with lots of artifacts on display. At the **Cleveland Corner** exhibit, you'll learn about Joe Hodge, the African American scout who lead Moses Cleaveland's group of settlers and surveyors to the area. He also served as Cleaveland's translator when talking with the Native American tribes.

**Kids participate in African dance at the Museum**

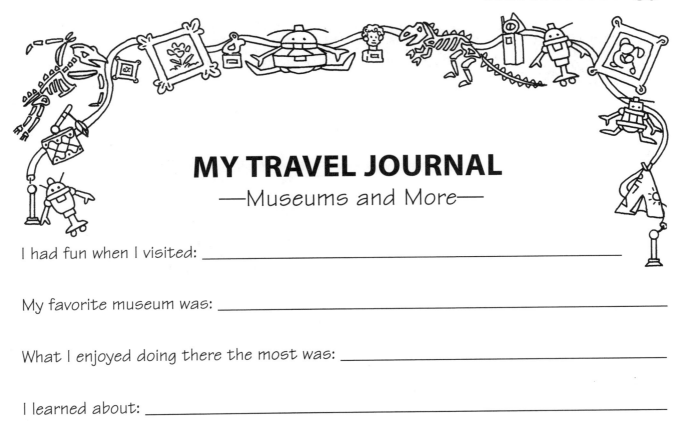

# MY TRAVEL JOURNAL
—Museums and More—

I had fun when I visited: _____

My favorite museum was: _____

What I enjoyed doing there the most was: _____

I learned about: _____

This is a picture of a painting or sculpture I saw

# THAT'S ENTERTAINMENT

A TRIP TO CLEVELAND ISN'T COMPLETE if you don't sample the area's fun spots. Fun can mean anything from riding roller coasters and carousels to playing miniature golf or driving bumper boats and go-carts. Or maybe you'd rather take batting practice, splash around a waterpark, and drive antique cars. Feel like more? You can ride a 1950s-style train through a national park. Or cruise up the Cuyahoga River on a triple-decker boat.

Even if the weather isn't sunny or warm, there is still plenty to do indoors. Several places offer indoor climbing mazes and game rooms. For six weeks every spring, Cleveland has an indoor amusement park with 150 attractions. The largest ride is a ten-story Ferris wheel with a glass top!

↑ The I-X Center becomes an amusement park once a year.

↑ Hold on tight at Cedar Point!

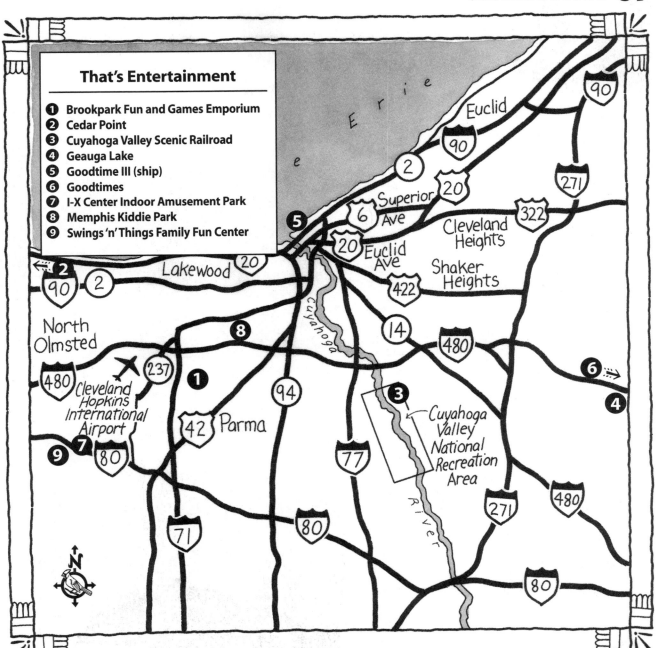

**That's Entertainment**

1. Brookpark Fun and Games Emporium
2. Cedar Point
3. Cuyahoga Valley Scenic Railroad
4. Geauga Lake
5. Goodtime III (ship)
6. Goodtimes
7. I-X Center Indoor Amusement Park
8. Memphis Kiddie Park
9. Swings 'n' Things Family Fun Center

# THE GOODTIME III

One of the best ways to discover Cleveland is by water. A two-hour cruise on the *Goodtime III* takes you through Cleveland Harbor and then up the Cuyahoga River. You can relax on one of three decks. Listen to the recorded narration as mellow-voiced Cleveland DJ Larry Morrow tells the history of Cleveland.

*Cuyahoga* is a Native American word for "crooked." The river snakes through the Flats' section of restaurants and nightclubs. It passes the **Lorenzo Carter Cabin**, home of Cleveland's first settler, and other important landmarks. But the most amazing part of your journey will be seeing the many different bridges that lift, turn, and rise to let the boat pass.

The *Goodtime III* leaves ⇧ from North Coast Harbor.

You'll see 19 different bridges on a *Goodtime III* cruise.

# BRIDGES, BRIDGES

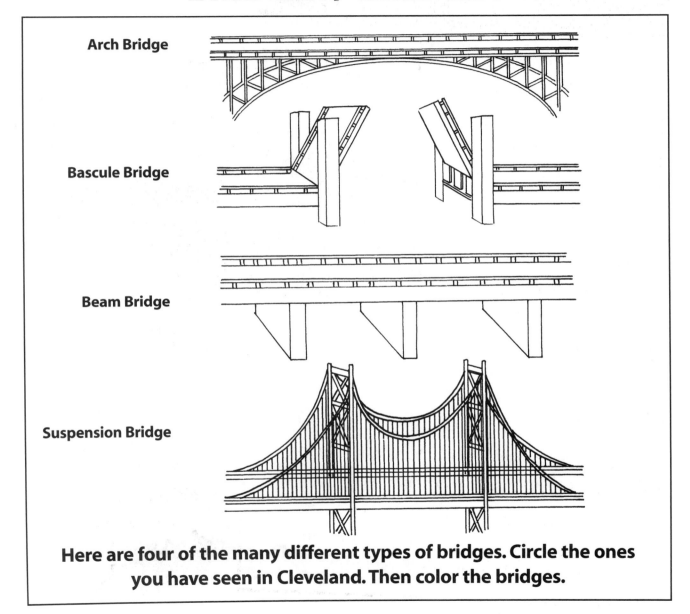

Arch Bridge

Bascule Bridge

Beam Bridge

Suspension Bridge

**Here are four of the many different types of bridges. Circle the ones you have seen in Cleveland. Then color the bridges.**

# CEDAR POINT

Attention all coaster-heads! If you love the thrills that only a roller coaster ride can give, Cedar Point is your kind of place. Cedar Point offers a world-record 12 roller coasters in all shapes and sizes.

The **Jr. Gemini** roller coaster doesn't allow adults unless they are accompanied by a youngster. This roller coaster goes 6 miles an hour and is perfect for kids who want a taste of the bigger coasters.

Not all of the 56 rides at Cedar Point leave your heart in your throat. There are carousels, paddlewheel boats, antique cars, and a sky ride.

In addition to the rides, enjoy the **Oceana Marine Complex** animal show stadium and aquarium, **Berenstain Bear Country** playland, **Kid Arthur's Court** playland, and a petting farm with 200 animals.

Cedar Point's newest attractions are Challenge Park (with a go-cart track and miniature golf course) and Soak City waterpark.

⇑ Get wet at Cedar Point's Soak City.

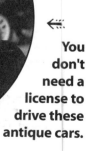

⇐ You don't need a license to drive these antique cars.

# MIXED-UP PICTURE STORY

**To find out what's happening at the amusement park, put the scene in the correct order by filling in the number box in the bottom corner of each picture. When you're done, color in the scene.**

# GEAUGA LAKE

Whether you like wet or dry fun, Geauga Lake has more than 100 attractions in its 278 acres. The park's two newest rides are the **Mind Eraser**, a boomerang-style roller coaster, and **Grizzly Run**, a white-water ride on an eight-person raft.

Geauga Lake was created way back in 1888, and many of the classic rides are still popular. The **Marcus Illions Carousel**, built in 1926, features 64 hand-carved wooden horses. And the **Flying Scooters** made its first run at the 1939 World's Fair.

**Turtle Beach** for kids has a combination of 11 slides, water chutes, and play areas. And everyone can enjoy getting sloshed around in **The Wave**, a massive wave pool that holds 2 million gallons of water.

**The Mind Eraser is only for the brave!** ⇧

**Geauga Lake takes its name from the park's 70-acre lake. The lake was created when a glacier scraped out a deep hole in the landscape.**

⇦

**There's plenty to do at Turtle Beach.**

# A DAY AT GEAUGA LAKE

**Without telling anyone what you're doing, ask for a word to fill in each blank. For example, "Give me an action word." When all the blanks have been filled in, read the story out loud. One blank has been filled in for you.**

When _____ turned _____ years old, his grandmother took him to
     boy's name 1       number

an amusement park. He was very happy. He went on the _____
                    describing word

rides, and he bought _____ foods from the vendors.
          describing word

    Grandma bought him a ticket for the ___**purple**___ Monster—the
              color

highest roller coaster in _____. He climbed into his seat and the ride
        state

began. _____ raised his hands into the air and screamed with
     boy's name 1

delight. "I love _____ amusement parks!" he yelled. When he got
      describing word

off the ride Grandma laughed. He looked happy, but his face was _____!
            color

# CUYAHOGA VALLEY SCENIC RAILROAD

↑ **A diesel locomotive pulls the train.**

All aboard! This train ride begins in Independence, a southeastern suburb of Cleveland. Choose your seat in a passenger car from the old New York Central or Santa Fe Railroads. The 1950s diesel locomotive will take you south through the Cuyahoga Valley National Recreation Area.

The Cuyahoga Valley Scenic Railroad offers a variety of trips. The **Scenic Limited** is a 90-minute round trip to the town of Peninsula. The **Peninsula Adventure** trip allows passengers to spend time in this historic village of shops and cafés. You can also rent bikes and ride on the national park's **Tow Path Trail**, which follows the Ohio & Erie Canal.

The **Valley Explorer** trip takes you on a nature tour through the Cuyahoga Valley National Recreation Area. A park ranger rides along to answer questions. The train stops so you get a chance to see wildlife. The ranger will even take you on a nature-trail hike.

↑ **Students enjoy touring the Cuyahoga Valley National Recreation Area.**

# COLOR TO FIND THE ANSWER

**If you see this sight, you'll want to get out of the way fast!**
**Color the shapes with numbers in them black.**
**Color the other shapes any colors you want.**

# FUN CENTERS

Cleveland has lots of fun centers. In Avon, **Goodtimes** has go-carts that are designed for a parent and toddler to drive together, as well as miniature golf, bumper boats, and batting cages.

**Swings 'n' Things Family Fun Center** in Olmsted Township is the largest family fun center in Ohio. The complex has a giant game room, go-carts, bumper boats, and batting cages. The two 18-hole miniature golf courses have clubs for kids.

**Memphis Kiddie Park** in Brooklyn features a merry-go-round, pony carts, a Ferris wheel, and a train.

**Brookpark Fun and Games Emporium** has two 18-hole miniature golf courses, go-carts, and a batting cage. For indoor fun there's a video arcade, skee ball machines, and a climbing room for kids under 4½ feet tall.

**Go-carts race around the track.**

**Wet and wild bumper boats** ⇛

# GOING FOR A HOLE IN ONE

**Can you get the ball in the hole? Sink the ball by completing the maze.**
**When you're done, color in the scene.**

# I-X CENTER INDOOR AMUSEMENT PARK

This former 20-acre tank factory is now a year-round convention center. But for 6 weeks a year, in April and May, the I-X Center becomes a huge indoor amusement park with more than 150 rides, games, shows, and special events. A permanent fixture in the park is a 10-story Ferris wheel—the world's tallest. The top of the wheel is covered by a glass-enclosed atrium which allows riders at the top to see the airport and the city beyond. The miniature golf, video arcade, and roller coaster are also popular attractions, and younger children stay busy with rides and a petting zoo.

⇧ **This Ferris wheel is 10 stories high.**

**Dozens of attractions sparkle**
**at the I-X.**

# MY TRAVEL JOURNAL
## —That's Entertainment—

These are the names of the places I visited: _____

My favorite place was: _____

The strangest thing I saw was: _____

This is a picture of something I saw

# 8 LET'S EAT!

WHETHER YOU ARE A FINICKY EATER or someone who enjoys exotic dishes, Cleveland has your kind of food.

How about a fast-food restaurant that serves perogies, a Polish version of ravioli? Try the pizza and spaghetti in the restaurants of Little Italy. Or you can eat seafood, chicken fingers, or hamburgers in one of the restaurants on the Cuyahoga River. Many serve kid-sized portions.

Several foods were invented here. Cleveland candy-maker Clarence Crane invented Life Savers, the candy with the hole in the center. The Stouffer's frozen food empire started out in 1922 as a family-run dairy bar in the Cleveland Arcade. Cleveland chemist Graham C. Clarke invented a way to put bubbles in a drink—now we call his invention a soft drink.

⬆ For restaurants galore, visit the Cleveland Arcade.

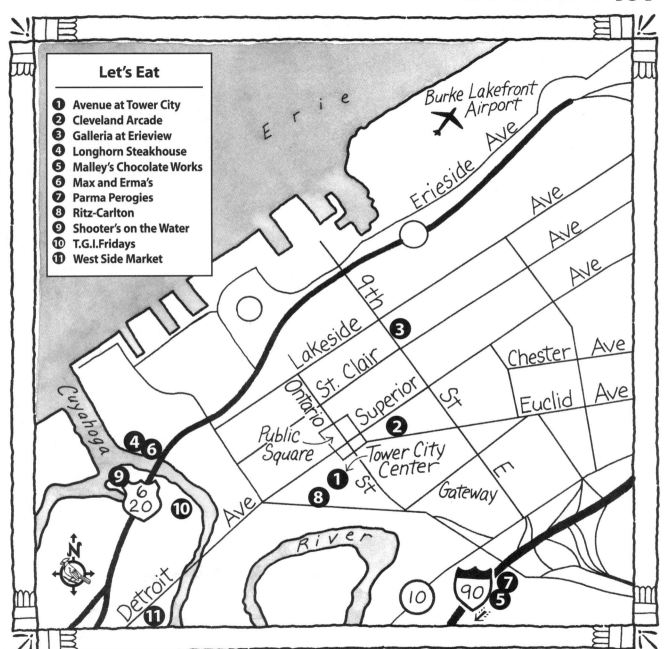

**Let's Eat**

1. Avenue at Tower City
2. Cleveland Arcade
3. Galleria at Erieview
4. Longhorn Steakhouse
5. Malley's Chocolate Works
6. Max and Erma's
7. Parma Perogies
8. Ritz-Carlton
9. Shooter's on the Water
10. T.G.I.Fridays
11. West Side Market

# DOWNTOWN EATS

On a busy day of sightseeing downtown, you may want to grab a quick bite at one of these places.

When the **Cleveland Arcade** was built in 1890, it was the first indoor shopping mall in the United States. This five-story building with brass railings and a glass ceiling is a National Historic Landmark. You can get a snack or eat lunch at one of the 20 eateries inside.

You can ride the rapid transit train to Tower City on Public Square and spend the day shopping at the **Avenue at Tower City**. This three-level indoor mall has shops, movie theaters, and an enormous food court. In warm weather, take your tray outside and eat on a balcony overlooking the Cuyahoga River.

⇡ **Holiday festivities at the Avenue at Tower City**

# HIDE AND SEEK!

**Draw a circle around each hidden object in this drawing of a Cleveland mall. When you're done, color in the scene. Look for: balloon, airplane, turtle, soda can, television, pizza slice, pencil, birthday cake, bug, ruler, top hat, baseball, boot, the planet Saturn, bowl**

# THE GALLERIA AT ERIEVIEW

The Galleria at Erieview is a 2-story mall with a curved glass ceiling and glass elevator. The food court has indoor dining or outdoor patio tables. The Galleria also has several fancier restaurants and many great stores for browsing.

Buy delicious candy at the **Malley's Chocolate Shop**, or wander through the baseball souvenirs and clothes at the **Cleveland Indians Team Shop**.

From Thanksgiving through the Christmas holidays, don't miss the Galleria's 60-foot Christmas tree. It's decorated with 77,000 lights and dozens of animated toy airplanes, wagons, and pinwheels. Three toy trains weave in and out of the tree's branches.

A shuttle leaves the Galleria every 20 minutes for the North Coast Harbor attractions located three blocks north.

⇧ Pick up something to eat at the Galleria food court.

# CROSSWORD FUN

**The mall is a great place to spend a rainy afternoon. Solve this crossword by figuring out the clues or completing the sentences. If you need some help, use the clue box**

## Across

2. The mall is a fun place to go with your _____.
5. Chocolate chip _____ make a great snack after a long day of shopping.
8. Ride this set of "moving stairs" to get to the second-floor stores.

## Down

1. If you want to buy things, put this in your wallet!
3. For lunch, stop at a _____.
4. Most malls have several theaters that show _____.
6. Put all of your purchases in a shopping ___.
7. You can find games, dolls, and fun things to do at the _____ store.

### Clue Box

| | |
|---|---|
| bag | money |
| cookies | movies |
| escalator | restaurant |
| friends | toy |

# PARMA PIEROGIES

To make your Cleveland visit complete, try this Polish fast-food restaurant. Pierogies, also called Polish ravioli, are the main course. Pierogies are pasta dumplings stuffed with your choice of fillings: potatoes, sauerkraut, broccoli and cheddar cheese, spinach and mozzarella cheese, mushrooms and swiss cheese, or cottage cheese and prunes.

Other Polish items on the menu are potato pancakes, kielbasa sausage, and stuffed cabbage. Try the Flamingo Pink Lemonade or sample the six dessert perogies stuffed with apple, apricot, blueberry, raspberry, cherry, or chocolate filling.

The restaurant has a large pink mascot named Pingo the Flamingo. You may get to shake his wing on your visit.

⇑
**The owner of Parma Pierogies, Mary Poldruhi, and her trademark flamingo**

# WHAT'S WRONG HERE?

**Not all is right at the chocolate factory today.**
**Circle at least 12 things that you think are wrong with this picture.**
**When you're done, color the scene.**

# FUN FOOD IN THE FLATS

**West Bank:**

**T.G.I. Fridays** is a chain restaurant that has fun food for all tastes and age groups. You can drive to **Shooter's on the Water,** or you can get there by boat. People dock their boats at the restaurant and dine on the multi-leveled deck overlooking the Cuyahoga River.

**East Bank:**

For a Wild West experience on the East Bank, try the **Longhorn Steakhouse.** Check out the saddles in the rafters and stuffed animals like the jackelope (a jackrabbit with horns).

    **Max and Erma's** has a hefty children's menu. Eat on the patio and sip an exotic drink such as Beetlejuice (grape juice and Sprite with three gummy worms) or an Oreo shake.

⇡ **Shooter's on the Water draws a crowd of boats.**

**If you don't have a boat, don't give up the ship. The Holy Moses Water Taxi (named for city founder Moses Cleaveland) ferries passengers across the river.**

# UNSCRAMBLE THE FOODS

**TSEKA**

**HCICKNE**

**DASAL**

**KEHAS**

**RERUMBHAG**

In this activity, unscramble each food word. When you have unscrambled the words, draw a line connecting each food to the correct picture.

# CHILDREN'S TEA AT THE RITZ-CARLTON

Have you ever wanted to sip tea from china cups and eat fancy cookies and sandwiches on china plates? The Ritz-Carlton Hotel serves a Children's Tea from 1:30 p.m. to 5 p.m. every Sunday in the lobby lounge. Kids enjoy special tea treats served on china plates. The tea is open to all youngsters, not just hotel guests. Waiters serve hot cocoa with whipped cream and marshmallows, warm spiced apple juice, and fruit-flavored sweet tea. If you prefer a cold drink, try the Ritz-Carlton Fruit Punch. Even the fancy finger sandwiches are kid-friendly, with American cheese, ham, or peanut butter and grape jelly. Top off tea with chocolate chip or teddy bear cookies, or fresh fruit tarts.

⬆ **Tea at the elegant Ritz-Carlton**

**For a different kind of birthday party, you can invite your friends to tea at the Ritz-Carlton!**

# WHAT'S IN COMMON?

**Each plate of tea and cookies has something in common with the two others in the same row. For example, in the top row, plates have the same pattern. Draw a line through each row and describe what the items in that row have in common. Don't forget diagonals!**

# WEST SIDE MARKET

An open-air market is much more fun than a grocery store. Take a trip to the West Side Market, where restaurant chefs and ordinary shoppers buy fruits, vegetables, baked goods, and meats.

The market is easy to find. Look for the Italian clock tower on one corner of the huge yellow brick building. Take your time wandering through the 180 stands. Smell the wonderful breads. Listen to the shouts of the vendors. Then go back and pick out the fruits, rolls, deli salads, meats, and cheeses you want for a picnic. When you're done, head north to Edgewater Park on Lake Erie for the freshest picnic you'll ever eat.

⬆ **Vendors offer fruits, vegetables, and much more.**

**Cleveland doctor James H. Salisbury invented the Salisbury steak.**

# WHAT'S THE DIFFERENCE?

**These two drawings of people enjoying the West Side Market might look the same, but they're not. Can you find at least 15 differences between the two scenes?**

# MALLEY'S CHOCOLATE FACTORY TOURS

Hear the history of how chocolate came to be the world's favorite flavor on this delicious tour. A trip through Malley's chocolate works allows you to see the various candy centers being dipped in chocolate. You'll also watch the chocolate molds being filled and see the chefs cooking candy in copper kettles over open flames. The nut shop tour shows you how the nuts are roasted, salted, and then dipped in chocolate. Best of all, Malley's generous samples make this tour as delicious as it is fun.

⇑ These tasty treats are almost ready for sampling.

In the specialty design center, chocolate designers make chocolate into pianos, vases, champagne glasses, and even Cinderella's slipper!

# MY TRAVEL JOURNAL
## —Let's Eat!—

These are the names of some of the restaurants I ate at:

_____

The most unusual food I ate was: _____

Mt least favorite food was: _____

This is a picture of one restaurant I visited.

# CALENDAR OF CLEVELAND EVENTS

*The special days celebrated in Cleveland represent a mix of the city's ethnic and cultural heritage. From neighborhood festivals and parades to the dozens of shows and activities at the I-X Center, there is never a break in the action.*

## January

### Martin Luther King Jr. Day Celebration

Cleveland, (216) 721-5722. Western Reserve Historical Society hosts a weekend of programs and activities to commemorate the civil rights leader's life and ideals.

### Mid-America Boat Show

Cleveland, (216) 621-3618. The I-X Center hosts a mammoth indoor boat show, the perfect antidote for all that snow outside.

### Winterscape

Cleveland, (216) 623-6393. The Sunday that falls 2 weeks after Christmas is a great day for an outdoor festival on Public Square. The 1-day family festival includes an ice-sculpting contest, penguins from Sea World, food vendors, and outdoor activities for kids. Winterscape is also the last day that the holiday ice rink on Public Square is open. Sponsored by the Greater Cleveland Growth Association.

## February

### Cleveland International Rod and Custom Auto-Rama

Cleveland, (216) 382-1616. Features over 400 vehicles and 150 commercial displays in the Cleveland Convention Center. The largest indoor car show in the Cleveland area is held on the first weekend in February.

### Black History Month

Cleveland, (216) 795-7070. Karamu Theatre celebrates the African American experience with two theatrical productions that depict the strength and determination of the African American community.

### Cleveland Indians Winterfest

CSU Convocation Center, (216) 420-4200.

### National Home & Garden Show

Cleveland, (216) 529-1300. This show at the I-X Center features the latest innovations from the construction and landscaping industries.

## March

### St. Patrick's Day Parade

Cleveland, (216) 777-2238. Everyone seems to be Irish when the St. Patrick's Day Parade winds its way through downtown Cleveland. The weather is usually overcast and cold, so bring a green snowsuit.

### Cleveland International Film Festival
Tower City, (216) 623-0400.

### Greater Cleveland Auto Show
Cleveland, (216) 328-1500. The I-X Center show features all the new makes and models for domestic and foreign cars.

### I-X Indoor Amusement Park
Cleveland, (216) 676-6000. The annual 6-week-long indoor amusement park at the I-X Center gets bigger every year.

## April

### Tri-C JazzFest
Cleveland, (216) 987-4400. Cuyahoga Community College hosts America's premier educational jazz festival. Jazzfest is 14 days of concerts and educational events throughout the city. The event draws international jazz artists and jazz lovers from all over the country.

## May

### Great American Rib Cook-off
Cleveland, (216) 247-2722. Chefs come from as far away as Texas and Australia to compete in the rib-cooking contest held at Burke Lakefront Airport.

### Urban League Black and White Gala Celebration
Cleveland,(216) 622-0999. Tenth anniversary black tie dinner dance at 7 p.m. in the Renaissance Hotel ballroom. This event highlights the positive relationships among the diverse communities in Greater Cleveland.

### Revco Fitness Expo and Revco-Cleveland Marathon & 10K Race
Cleveland, (216) 425-9811. This annual downtown race in early May draws thousands of participants from all over the world. In 1996, a world's best road record was set for the 10K race.

## June

### Parade the Circle Celebration
University Circle, (216) 421-7340, ext. 297. A multicultural art parade with giant puppets, colorful costumes, original dance and music ensembles, and floats you will never see in a conventional parade. The first Saturday in June.

↑ **Parade the Circle Celebration**

### The Marilyn Bianchi Kids' Playwriting Festival
Cleveland Heights, (216) 932-6838. Dobama Theatre sponsors an annual playwriting contest for

Cuyahoga County students in the first through twelfth grades. During the first weekend in June the plays are staged free to the public.

### Summerfare

Cleveland, (216) 623-6393. Every Friday at noon in June, July, and August, there is a Lunchbox Rock series of free concerts on Public Square. Area rock groups perform. Bring a lunch and eat outdoors.

## July

### GTE Mobilenet Cleveland Cool Kidsfest

Cleveland, (216) 247-2722. A festival of children's activities held at Nautica Entertainment Complex.

### Cleveland Orchestra Concert

Cleveland, (216) 231-7300. This Cleveland Orchestra Concert held on Public Square is free to the public.

### Festival of Freedom

Edgewater Park's spectacular fireworks display. People watch this show either on land or from their boats.

## August

### Cuyahoga County Fair

Berea, (216) 243-0900. The Cuyahoga County Fair is a giant-sized, old-fashioned county fair with 4-H exhibits, livestock judging, and a midway with fair food, carnival rides, and games.

### NAACP/Urban League Family Picnic Day

Cleveland, (216) 622-0999. The public is welcome to join the picnic on the first Saturday in August at Luke Easter Park. A fun-filled family event that recognizes and celebrates the contributions of the African American family.

⇡ **The Cleveland National Air Show**

## September

### Cleveland National Air Show

North Coast Harbor, (216) 781-7469. This air show is one of the country's oldest and best annual shows. It takes place at the Burke Lakefront Airport.

### Hispanic Heritage Month

Cleveland, (216) 664-2220.

### Johnny Appleseed Festival

Brunswick, (330) 225-5577. This event features delicious apple desserts and many special activities.

### Old World Oktoberfest

Geauga Lake, (216) 562-7131. For two weekends, Geauga Lake has an annual German festival with attractions for all age groups: bands, ice sculpting, dance contests, and German foods from bratwurst to strudel. The music ranges from polka and rock to oldies and country. All park rides are open for the event.

## October

### Cleveland Ski & Winter Sports Fair

Cleveland, (216) 676-6000. The I-X Center hosts a show featuring the latest in ski equipment and other winter sports equipment and clothing.

### Hale Harvest Festival

Bath, (800) 589-9703. Hale Farm and Village is transformed into a picture-postcard scene of harvest bounty during the annual festival.

## November

### Downtown Holiday Lighting Program

Cleveland, (216) 623-6393. The day after Thanksgiving is the annual downtown holiday lighting ceremony on Public Square. During the day, there are clowns, mimes, and balloon folders. After dark, Santa arrives with a flourish, carols are sung, and the holiday lights are turned on. Area figure-skating clubs perform, and then the Public Square skating rink is opened to the public. There is a $3 fee for ice skating. Skate rental is $1.

⇡ **Holiday lighting ceremony at Public Square**

### Thanksgiving Polka Weekend

Cleveland, (216) 692-1000 or (800) 800-5981. Held in the Marriott Key Center hotel downtown, this annual 3-day polkafest features 20 polka bands. Polka enthusiasts come from all over the U.S. and Canada to hear the bands perform. On Saturday there is the annual Polka Award show at the National Cleveland-Style Polka Hall of Fame in Euclid. Saturday night includes a Polka Mass at 6 p.m. and then a Meet-the-Winner dance at 7 p.m. in the ballroom of the Marriott Key Center.

## December

### Downtown Skating on Public Square

Cleveland, (216) 623-6393. The Public Square

ice-skating rink remains open throughout the holidays from noon to 10 p.m. Some people who work in downtown Cleveland enjoy skating on their lunch hour. There is a $3 fee for skating. Skate rental is $1.

### Black Nativity

Cleveland, (216) 795-7077. The Karamu Performing Arts Theatre presents an annual staging of the Langston Hughes' play. *Black Nativity* is an African American celebration of the Christmas story that combines gospel music with dance and costumes. This play has become as much a part of the Cleveland Christmas tradition as the *Nutcracker* and *A Christmas Carol.*

### Medieval Feasts & Spectacles

Cleveland, (216) 579-9745. Held at Trinity Cathedral, these events include four evenings of authentic fourteenth-century food and entertainment held in the nave of Trinity Cathedral on East 22nd Street and Euclid Avenue in downtown Cleveland. You get to eat with your fingers and you can wear a medieval costume if you want. Cost is $40 a night, which goes to benefit the Brown Bag music concerts that take place at Trinity Cathedral every Wednesday at noon from October through May.

### Rock and Roll Shoot Out

Cleveland, (216) 420-2000. College Basketball in Gund Arena.

# RESOURCE GUIDE: WHEN, WHAT, AND HOW MUCH?

*Even though all the sites listed in this guide have programs for kids and families, not every program offered by these places is suitable. Before buying tickets, have your parents check to see that the program is OK for you to see. Also remember that dates, times, and places listed in the Resource Guide change from year to year, so it might be a good idea to call ahead before you visit.*

## If You Get Lost

Do you know what to do if you get lost? When you first arrive at the site, make a plan with your parents about what to do if you lose them. If you forget that plan, don't panic. Try to retrace your steps. Then, stop at the nearest, safest place possible, such as a checkout counter or security booth. Your first option is to call the place where you're staying and see if your parents have called. Then, explain your situation to someone who looks trustworthy: a museum volunteer, a store manager, or the police.

If there is an emergency and you need the police, fire department, or an ambulance, call 911 from any phone. You don't need coins.

## Important Numbers

Injury, accident, or emergency, 911
Cleveland Police, 911
Convention and Visitors Bureau of Greater Cleveland, (216) 623-4499
Poison Control Center, (216) 231-4455
Ohio State Highway Patrol for Cuyahoga County, (216) 587-4305

## Transportation

Budget, (216) 932-2134
Hertz, (216) 267-8900
Thrifty, (216) 267-6811
Dollar, (216) 267-3133
Americab, Inc., (216) 429-1111
Yellow Cab Company of Cleveland, (216) 623-1550
AMTRAK, (800) 872-7245. Daily downtown passenger train service located on the south shoreway between West 3rd and East 9th streets. The station is open Monday through Saturday, midnight to 3:30 p.m.
Greyhound Bus Lines, 1465 Chester Avenue, (800) 231-2222 for fares and schedule. The bus terminal is open 24 hours a day.
*Lakefront Lines,* (216) 267-8810. Charter bus or group tours available.

## Attractions

**The African American Museum**, 1765 Crawford Road, northwest of University Circle; (216) 791-1700. Open Tuesday through Friday, 10 a.m. to 3 p.m.; Saturday, 11 a.m. to 3 p.m. Admission is $2 for children under age 17, $3 for adults.

**The Arcade**, 401 Euclid Avenue; (216) 621-8500. You can enter the block-long building from Superior or Euclid Avenues. Open Monday through Friday, 7 a.m. to 7 p.m.; Saturday, 7:15 a.m. to 6:45 p.m. Closed on Sunday.

**Avenue at Tower City**, 50 Public Square; (216) 771-0033. The avenue of shops, restaurants, and movies is open Monday through Saturday, 10 a.m. to 8 p.m.; Sunday, noon to 6 p.m.

**Brookpark Fun and Games Emporium**, 6770 Brookpark Road, South Cleveland; (216) 351-1910. Open Monday through Thursday, 11 a.m. to 10 p.m.; Friday and Saturday, 11 a.m. to 11 p.m.; Sunday, noon to 10 p.m. Admission is $5 for 25 tokens. Go-carts are $4 for 5 minutes.

**Burnette's Farm & Educational Center**, 6940 Columbia Road, Olmsted Township; (216) 235-4050. Reservations recommended. Open Tuesday through Saturday, 10 a.m. to 11 a.m. and 2 p.m. to 3 p.m.; Sunday, 2 p.m. to 3 p.m. Closed on Monday. Admission is $4 for kids, $5 for adults.

**Cedar Point**, 1 Causeway Drive, Sandusky, Ohio 44871-5006; (419) 627-2350. Located midway between Cleveland and Toledo in Sandusky, Ohio. Take the Ohio Turnpike (I-80) to Exit 7 and follow the signs north on U.S. 250, or take Exit 6A and follow Route 4 north. Opens at 10 a.m. Call for closing times. Admission varies according to age and height. Admission is $29 for people ages 4 to 59; $7 for kids age 4 and younger.

**Cleveland Ballet**, One Playhouse Square, 1375 Euclid Avenue, Suite 330; (216) 621-2260. Call for a schedule of performances and times.

**Cleveland Botanical Gardens**, 11030 East Boulevard, University Circle; (216) 721-1600. Open outdoors from dawn to dusk. Open indoors Monday through Friday, 9 a.m. to 5 p.m.; Saturday, noon to 5 p.m.; Sunday, 1 p.m. to 5 p.m. Admission is free.

**Cleveland Cavaliers**, Gund Arena, One Center Court, Cleveland; (216) 420-2287. National Basketball Association season runs from November through April. Ticket prices are $10 to $51.

↑ **Lake Farmpark**

**Cleveland Children's Museum,** 1073 Euclid Avenue, University Circle; (216) 791-5437. School year hours: Closed Monday. Open Tuesday through Friday, 9 a.m. to 5 p.m.; Saturday, 10 a.m. to 5 p.m.; Sunday, noon to 5 p.m. Summer hours: Monday through Friday, 11 a.m. to 5 p.m.; Saturday, 10 a.m. to 5 p.m.; Sunday, 1 p.m. to 5 p.m. Admission is $4 for kids ages 2 to 15, $5 for adults age 16 and older.

**Cleveland Crunch,** Cleveland State University Convocation Center, 2000 Prospect Avenue, Cleveland 44115; (216) 687-5082. Tickets cost $11 to $18 at the Convocation Center box office. Call for game schedule and times. Tickets also available through Ticketmaster locations at (216) 241-5555.

**Cleveland Indians,** Jacobs Field, 2401 Ontario Street; (216) 420-4200. Call for game times and admission. To arrange a tour of Jacobs Field, call the Cleveland Indians Community Relations Department at (216) 420-4400.

**Clevelend Lumberjacks,** One Center Ice, 200 Huron Road; (216) 420-0000. Home games in Gund Arena run from October through May. Tickets for adults are $10 to $20. Kids age 17 and under get a $2 discount.

**Cleveland Metroparks,** administrative offices are at 4101 Fulton Parkway in Cleveland; (216) 351-6300. A map of Cleveland Metroparks is available free at any nature center or park office or by mail. Other phone numbers: Ranger Headquarters, 9301 Pearl Road in Strongsville, (216) 243-7860; Swimming, (216) 351-6300; Winter Recreation

↑ **Terminal Tower and sculpture**

Information Line, (216) 351-6300; Picnic Area Reservations and Permits, (216) 351-6300.

**Cleveland Metroparks Zoo & Rain Forest,** 3900 Brookside Park Drive; (216) 661-6500. Open year round. Zoo is open daily, 9 a.m. to 5 p.m.; Rain Forest, 10 a.m. to 5 p.m. Extended summer weekend hours from Memorial Day through Labor Day are 9 a.m. to 7 p.m. Admission to Zoo and Rain Forest is $4 for kids ages 2 to 11, $7 for adults.

**Cleveland Museum of Art,** 11150 East Boulevard, University Circle; (216) 421-7340. Open Tuesday, Thursday, and Friday, 10 a.m. to 5:45 p.m.; Wednesday, 10 a.m. to 9:45 p.m.; Saturday, 9 a.m. to 4:45 p.m.; Sunday, 1 p.m. to 5:45 p.m. Closed Monday. Admission is free.

**Cleveland Museum of Natural History,** 1 Wade Oval Drive, University Circle; (216) 231-4600. Open Monday through Saturday, 10 a.m. to 5 p.m.;

Sunday, noon to 5 p.m. Open Wednesday until 10 p.m. Admission is $4 for kids ages 5 to 17. Admission is free Tuesday and Thursday, 3 p.m. to 5 p.m.

**Cleveland Polo Club**, Route 87, east of Chagrin River Road, (216) 441-1804. Tickets are $5 for adults, free for kids age 12 and under.

**Cleveland Orchestra**, Severance Hall, 11001 Euclid Avenue, University Circle; (216) 231-7300. Box office hours are Monday through Friday, 9 a.m. to 5 p.m. Call (216) 231-1111 or (800) 686-1141. The orchestra's summer home is Blossom Music Center. The ticket office is open Friday through Sunday, 1 p.m. to 5 p.m.

**Cleveland Public Library**, 325 Superior Avenue, (216) 623-2822. Open Monday through Saturday, 9 a.m. to 6 p.m.; Sunday, 1 p.m. to 5 p.m. Admission is free.

⬆ **Biking by the lake**

**Cuyahoga Valley National Recreation Area**, 15610 Vaughn Road, Brecksville. For more information or a map, call (216) 524-1497 or (800) 445-9667. The park will send you a free four-color map of the park that lists activities and will help you plan your visit.

**Cuyahoga Valley Scenic Railroad**, 1630 W. Mill Street, Peninsula, Ohio 44264; (800) 468-4070. Kids' tickets are $5 to $12; adult tickets are $7 to $20.

**DanceCleveland**, 1148 Euclid Avenue, Playhouse Square, Downtown; (216) 861-2213. Call 861-2213 for DanceCleveland's current season schedule.

**Discovery Zones**, East Cleveland locations: Golden Gate Shopping Center, 6420 Mayfield Road, (216) 461-8887; Great Lakes Mall, 78750 Mentor Avenue, (216) 974-8500. Open Sunday through Thursday, 10 a.m. to 8 p.m.; Friday and Saturday, 10 a.m. to 10 p.m. Admission is $6 for kids age 3 and older. Admission is free for adults.

**Flats Restaurants**
  **West Bank:**
    **T.G.I. Friday**, Powerhouse, 2000 Sycamore Street, (216) 621-1993
    **Shooter's on the Water**, 1148 Main Avenue, (216) 861-6900

  **East Bank:**
    **Longhorn Steakhouse**, 1058 Old River Road, (216) 623-1880
    **Landry's Seafood House**, 1036 Old River

Road, (216) 566-1010

**Max and Erma's**, 1106 Old River Road, (216) 771-8338

**Fagan's**, 996 Old River Road, (216) 241-6116

**The Holy Moses Water Taxi**, (216) 999-1625

**The Galleria at Erieview**, East 9th Street and St. Clair; (216) 621-9999. Open Monday through Friday, 10 a.m. to 7:30 p.m.; Saturday, 10 a.m. to 7 p.m.; Sunday, noon to 5 p.m.

**Geauga Lake**, 1060 N. Aurora Road, (Ohio Route 43, 9 miles north of Ohio Turnpike Exit 13); (216) 562-7131 or (800) 843-9283. Open daily May through September, 10 a.m. to 7 p.m. Admission is $20 for those taller than 48 inches. Children under 48 inches are $6.

*Goodtime III*, East Ninth Street Pier, North Coast Harbor; (216) 861-5110. From mid-June to September, 2-hour narrated boat cruises are available at noon and 3 p.m., 7 days a week. The *Goodtime III* also offers a 6 p.m. cruise on Sunday. Admission is $6 for kids ages 2 to 11, $10 for adults.

**Great Lakes Science Center**, 601 Erieside Avenue; (216) 694-2000. Open daily, 9:30 a.m. to 5:30 p.m. Omnimax Theater is open Wednesday through Saturday, 10 a.m. to 8 p.m.; Friday and Saturday, 11 a.m. to 7 p.m. Call for admission prices.

**Hale Farm and Village**, 2686 Oak Hill Road in Bath; (216) 575-9137. Open from May through October. Open Wednesday through Saturday,

↑ **This statue is one of the "Guardians of Traffic" on the Hope Memorial Bridge.**

10 a.m. to 5 p.m.; Sunday, noon to 5 p.m. Admission is $4.50 for kids ages 6 to 12, $7.50 for adults.

**The Health Museum**, 8911 Euclid Avenue, University Circle; (216) 231-5010. Open Monday through Friday, 9 a.m. to 5 p.m.; Saturday, 10 a.m. to 5 p.m.; Sunday, noon to 5 p.m. Admission is $2 for kids ages 6 to 17; $3.50 for adults.

**Holden Arboretum**, 9500 Sperry Road; (216) 256-1110 or (216) 946-4400. Open Tuesday through Sunday, 10 a.m. to 5 p.m. Admission is $1.75 for kids ages 6 to 12; $2.50 for adults.

**I-X Center Indoor Amusement Park**, I-X Center, 6200 Riverside Drive west of Hopkins Airport;

(216) 676-6000. Open for six weeks in April and May. Call for specific days and hours. Admission is $12.

**Karamu Performing Arts Theatre Center**, 2355 E. 89th Street; (216) 795-7077. Call for upcoming family productions, times, dates, and costs.

**Lake Erie Nature and Science Center**, 28728 Wolf Road, Bay Village; (216) 871-2900. Open Sunday through Friday, 1 p.m. to 5 p.m.; Saturday, 10 a.m. to 5 p.m. Planetarium hours are Sunday, 3 p.m. Admission is free. Planetarium show is $1 for kids age 12 and under, $2 for adults.

**Lake Farmpark**, 8800 Chardon Road, Kirtland; (216) 256-2122 or (800) 366-3276. Open daily, 9 a.m. to 5 p.m. Admission is $3.50 for ages 2 to 11, $5 for adults.

**Lolly the Trolley Tours of Cleveland**, tours start at Burke Lakefront Airport or Power House on the west bank of the Flats; (216) 579-6160. One or 2-hour narrated tours. Call for ticket costs.

**Malley's Chocolate Factory Tours**, 13400 Brookpark Road Cleveland; (800) 835-5684. Open Monday through Friday, 10 a.m. to 3 p.m. Admission is $1 for age 12 and under, $2 for people over age 12. Tours are 30 to 45 minutes long.

**Memphis Kiddie Park**, 10340 Memphis Avenue, Brooklyn; (216) 941-5995. Open weekdays from June through August, 10 a.m. to 9 p.m.; Friday through Sunday, 10 a.m. to 9:30 p.m. Open week-days from September through May, 10 a.m. to 8 p.m.; Friday through Sunday, 10 a.m. to 9 p.m. Rides are one ticket each. Tickets are 70 cents each; 10 for $6.50; 25 for $12. Admission to the park is free.

**National Cleveland-Style Polka Hall of Fame**, Shore Cultural Center, 291 E. 22nd Street, in Euclid; (216) 261-3263. Open Monday, Thursday, Friday, and Saturday, 10 a.m. to 2 p.m.; Tuesday, 3 p.m. to 8 p.m. Closed Sunday and Wednesday. Admission is free.

**Parma Pierogies**, two locations. West side: 7707 W. Ridgewood Drive, Parmatown Plaza in Parma; (216) 888-1200. Open Monday through Thursday, 11 a.m. to 10 p.m.; Friday and Saturday, 11 a.m. to 11 p.m.; Sunday, 1 p.m. to 7 p.m. East side: 5445

⚐ **Cleveland's skyline includes the Rock and Roll Hall of Fame and Great Lakes Science Center.**

Mayfield Road in Lyndhurst; (216) 449-2000. Open Monday through Thursday, 11 a.m. to 9 p.m.; Friday and Saturday, 11 a.m. to 10 p.m.; Sunday, 11 a.m. to 7 p.m.

**Ritz-Carlton Hotel**, 1515 W. 3rd Street, Cleveland; (216) 623-1300. Call for room rates and availability.

**Rock and Roll Hall of Fame and Museum**, One Key Plaza, North Coast Harbor; (216) 781-7625. On weekends and during holiday and summer seasons, reserve tickets in advance by calling (800) 493-7655. Open from Memorial Day through Labor Day, Sunday through Tuesday, 10 a.m. to 5:30 p.m.; Wednesday through Saturday 10 a.m. to 9 p.m. Open from Labor Day through Memorial Day, Thursday through Tuesday, 10 a.m. to 5:30 p.m.; Wednesday, 10 a.m. to 9 p.m. Admission is $9.50 for children ages 4 to 11, $13 for adults.

**Rockefeller Park Greenhouse**, 750 E. 88th Street, University Circle; (216) 664-3103. Open daily, 10 a.m. to 4 p.m. Admission is free.

**Sea World**, 1100 Sea World Drive (off Ohio Route 43) in Aurora; (800) 637-4268. Open daily May through September, 10 a.m. Call for closing times. Admission is $26 for adults and $20 for ages 3 to 11. Free admission for kids age 3 and under. Parking is $4 per vehicle.

**Steamship *William Mather* Museum**, North Coast Harbor; (216) 574-6262. Open May through

October. Admission is $2.50 for kids age 12 and under, $4.50 for adults.

**Swings 'n' Things**, 8501 Stearns Road, Olmsted Township; (216) 235-4420. Open mid-March through mid-October, Monday through Friday, noon to 11 p.m.; Saturday and Sunday, 11 a.m. to 11 p.m. Prices vary.

**Trolleyville U.S.A.**, 7100 Columbia Road, Olmstead Township; (216) 235-4725. Open May through November, 10 a.m. to 3 p.m. on Wednesday and Friday; noon to 5 p.m. on Saturday, Sunday, and holidays. Call to find out about special events. Admission is $2 for kids ages 3 to 11, $4 for adults.

**Terminal Tower Observation Deck**, 42nd floor of the Terminal Tower, 50 Public Square; (216) 771-0033. Open Saturday and Sunday, 11 a.m. to 4:30 p.m. Admission to the observation deck is $2 for adults and $1 for ages 5 to 16. Under age 5 is free.

**USS Cod**, 1089 East Ninth Street, North Coast Harbor; (216) 566-8770. Located between the William Mather Museum and Burke Lakefront Airport. Open daily May through September, 10 a.m. to 5 p.m. Admission is $2 for kids ages 1 to 12, $4 for adults.

**West Side Market**, 1995 W. 25th Street; (216) 664-3386. Open Monday, Wednesday, Friday, and Saturday. Open Monday and Wednesday, 7 a.m. to 4 p.m.; Friday and Saturday, 7 a.m. to 6 p.m.

# ANSWERS TO PUZZLES

## page 9

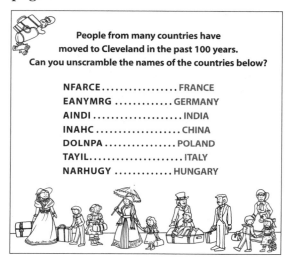

People from many countries have moved to Cleveland in the past 100 years. Can you unscramble the names of the countries below?

NFARCE.................FRANCE
EANYMRG ............GERMANY
AINDI....................INDIA
INAHC...................CHINA
DOLNPA................POLAND
TAYIL....................ITALY
NARHUGY ............HUNGARY

## page 17

FINISH

## page 19

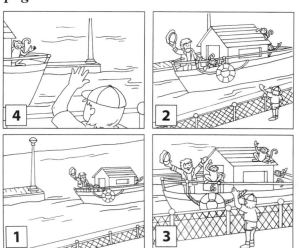

## page 21

*page 23*

```
B O N A T K M E H O R S E P V S H
L P H F G D Q S Y M H E B A O C H
A Y N L R G A I N N P T S B L H F
C T P C O B B L E S T O N E L O D
K A T W C M N R D V C E N T E O N
S E U E E D F N G N N O B T Y L Y
M D S R R U N N H B I U Y U B W R
I A X S Y C I N A K C L M R G D W
T O N P U K R N W B O A T F L G T
H I O E I S K R S A W M I L L U Y
R H T B L K I T E U L I M Y N F S
S Y D H C C H U R C H S B E E Q R
```

*page 25*

*page 33*

*page 35*

page 37

page 41

page 47

page 49

*page 51*

```
K O Q U I E T E C O P M Y P V U H
H P H B R D Q S O M H L E A R N H
D Y N O S G A I M A G A Z I N E F
E T P O D R S D P T R N G U L U D
S A T K G M E R U V E E N T E D N
K Y U E M A F N T N S O G C Y E Y
D R A R S R R U N N E U Y H B W R
S A X S P C I N R K A L M A A D W
P R N D C K R O W B R A T I L Q T
U B S E I A U R N P C D N R L U B
R I T B L K R T E U H I M Y N F S
D L D N I O P D I C T I O N A R Y
```

*page 53*

*page 61*

BALLS

BACKWARD
HAT

BATS

STRIPED
HATS

FRECKLES

GIRLS    HATS    STARS

*page 63*

*page 65*

|   | ¹P |   |   |   |   |   |   |   |
|---|----|---|----|---|---|---|---|---|
| ²C | O | U | ³R | T |   |   |   |   |
|   | I |   | E |   | ⁴W |   |   |   |
|   | N |   | ⁵A | N | T | H | E | M |
| ⁶N | E | T | S |   | A |   |   |   |
|   | S |   | M |   | M |   |   |   |
|   |   |   |   |   | M |   |   |   |
|   |   |   | ⁷B | E | N | C | ⁸H |   |
|   |   |   | R |   |   |   | O |   |
|   |   |   |   |   |   |   | O |   |
|   |   |   |   |   |   |   | P |   |
|   |   |   |   |   |   |   | S |   |

*page 67*

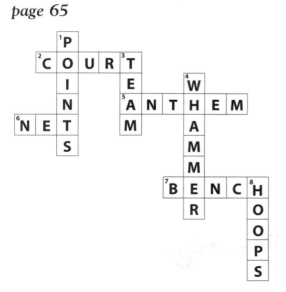

## page 73

```
K O N A T K M E S O P M Y P T U H
H E H F R D Q S Y M H E B A H N H
N L N L S G A I N N P T S B E N F
T E X P E R I M E N T N G U A U D
R C T W G M A R D V C E N T D E M
D T U E M D F N G N N C G T E E A
E R S R L U G N H U I N Y E R W G
S I X E P C F N D K C E M R A D N
P C Z D U K U O O M N I M A X Q E
U I S E I S N R N P Y C N L L U T
R O T B L K I T E U L S M Y N F S
A T O M S O P Y F W E A T H E R R
```

## page 75

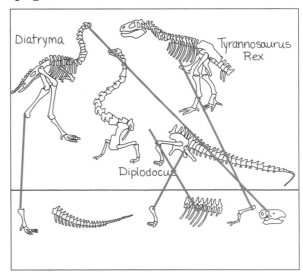

## page 77

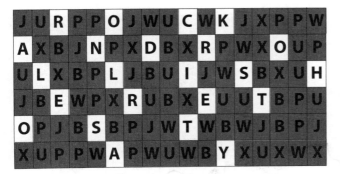

**Write the hidden message here:**

**ROCK AND ROLL IS HERE TO STAY**

## page 79

*page 83*

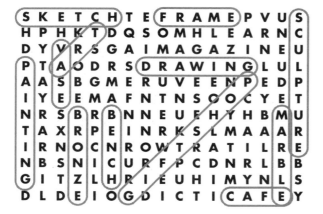

*page 91*

*page 95*

*page 97*

*page 103*

*page 105*

*page 107*

*page 109*

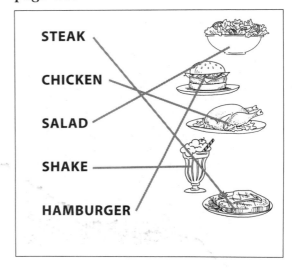

*page 111*

*page 113*

# GEOGRAPHICAL INDEX: WHERE IS EVERYTHING?

# INDEX

---

# PHOTO CREDITS

Pages i, iii (left), 90 (both)—Dan Feicht/Cedar Point; Page ii—Diana McNeese/Cleveland Playhouse; Pages iii (right), 28, 42 (both)—Sea World of Ohio; Page 1—Michael Evans/The Image Finders; Pages 2, 4, 8, 12, 14, 16, 24 (both), 44, 48 (top), 54, 60, 68, 70, 72, 74, 76, 78, 80, 98 (both), 102, 104, 112, 116, 118, 119, 124, 126—©Jonathan Wayne/216.361-1988;  Pages 3, 10—Western Reserve Historical Society; Page 6—River's Bend Parks Corporation; Page 18—Tom Cawley/National Park Service; Page 20—Holden Arboretum; Page 22 (both)—Hale Farm & Village; Page 26 (both)—M. Heffernan/Cleveland Botanical Gardens; Page 30 (both)—Lake Erie Nature & Science Center; Page 32—Cleveland Museum of Natural History; Page 34 (both)—Sanford Gross/Cleveland Metroparks Zoo; Page 36—Casey Batule/Cleveland Metroparks Zoo; Page 38—Dr. Jim Burnette; Pages 40, 122—Lake Farmpark; Page 46—Trolley Tours of Cleveland; Pages 48 (bottom), 58, 74, 100—Jim Baron/The Image Finders; Page 50—Jennie Jones/Cleveland Public Library; Page 52—Roger Mastroianni/The Image Finders; Page 56 (both)—Roger Mastroianni/Cleveland Orchestra; Page 62 (both)—Tom Rudo/Lumberjacks; Page 64—Lou Capozzola/NBA; Page 66 (both)—Cleveland Crunch; Page 68—Ian Adams/National Park Service; Page 82 (both)—G.M. Donley/Cleveland Museum of Art; Page 84—African American Museum; Page 86—Cedar Point; Page 86—I-X Amusement Park; Page 88—Captain Jack C. Wagner; Page 92 (both)—Geauga Lake; Page 94 (both)—National Park Service; Page 96 (both)—Swings & Things; Page 106—Parma Pierogies; Page 108—Mort Tucker; Page 110—Ritz Carlton; Page 114—Malley Chocolate Factory; Page 123—Mark E. Gibson/The Image Finders; Page 125—Scott Pease/The Image Finders.

### American Origins Series

Each is 48 pages and $12.95 hardcover.
**Tracing Our English Roots**
**Tracing Our German Roots**
**Tracing Our Irish Roots**
**Tracing Our Italian Roots**
**Tracing Our Japanese Roots**
**Tracing Our Jewish Roots**
**Tracing Our Polish Roots**

### Bizarre & Beautiful Series

Each is 48 pages, $14.95 hardcover, $9.95 paperback.
**Bizarre & Beautiful Ears**
**Bizarre & Beautiful Eyes**
**Bizarre & Beautiful Feelers**
**Bizarre & Beautiful Noses**
**Bizarre & Beautiful Tongues**

### Extremely Weird Series

Each is 32 pages and $5.95 paperback.
**Extremely Weird Animal Defenses**
**Extremely Weird Animal Disguises**
**Extremely Weird Animal Hunters**
**Extremely Weird Bats**
**Extremely Weird Endangered Species**
**Extremely Weird Fishes**
**Extremely Weird Frogs**
**Extremely Weird Reptiles**
**Extremely Weird Spiders**
**Extremely Weird Birds**
**Extremely Weird Insects**
**Extremely Weird Mammals**
**Extremely Weird Micro Monsters**
**Extremely Weird Primates**
**Extremely Weird Sea Creatures**
**Extremely Weird Snakes**

### Kidding Around™ Travel Series

Each is 144 pages and $7.95 paperback.
**Kidding Around Atlanta**
**Kidding Around Cleveland**
**Kids Go! Denver**
**Kidding Around Minneapolis/St. Paul**
**Kidding Around San Francisco**
**Kids Go! Seattle**
**Kidding Around Washington, D.C.**

### Kids Explore Series

Written by kids for kids, each is $9.95 paperback.
**Kids Explore America's African American Heritage**, 160 pages
**Kids Explore America's Hispanic Heritage**, 160 pages
**Kids Explore America's Japanese American Heritage**, 160 pages
**Kids Explore America's Jewish Heritage**, 160 pages
**Kids Explore the Gifts of Children with Special Needs**, 128 pages
**Kids Explore the Heritage of Western Native Americans**, 128 pages

### Masters of Motion Series

Each is 48 pages and $6.95 paperback.
**How to Drive an Indy Race Car**
**How to Fly a 747**
**How to Fly the Space Shuttle**

### Rainbow Warrior Artists Series

Each is 48 pages, $14.95 hardcover, $9.95 paperback.
**Native Artists of Africa**
**Native Artists of Europe**
**Native Artists of North America**

### Rough and Ready Series

Each is 48 pages and $4.95 paperback.
**Rough and Ready Homesteaders**
**Rough and Ready Cowboys**
**Rough and Ready Loggers**
**Rough and Ready Outlaws and Lawmen**
**Rough and Ready Prospectors**
**Rough and Ready Railroaders**

### X-ray Vision Series

Each is 48 pages and $6.95 paperback.
**Looking Inside the Brain**
**Looking Inside Cartoon Animation**
**Looking Inside Caves and Caverns**
**Looking Inside Sports Aerodynamics**
**Looking Inside Sunken Treasure**
**Looking Inside Telescopes and the Night Sky**

### Other Children's Titles

**Habitats: Where the Wild Things Live**, 48 pages, $9.95

**The Indian Way: Learning to Communicate with Mother Earth**, 112 pages, $9.95

### Ordering Information

Please check your local bookstore for our books, or call **1-800-888-7504** to order direct and to receive a complete catalog. A shipping charge will be added to your order total.

Send all inquiries to:
**John Muir Publications**
**P.O. Box 613, Santa Fe, NM 87504**